jcore

JCORE works within the Jewish community to raise awareness of racism and to encourage active involvement in building a cohesive and inclusive society.

JCORE works on three fronts:

- **Race equality education**
  We work with all age groups to raise awareness and combat racism

- **Black-Asian-Jewish dialogue**.
  We engage with other minority ethnic groups and communities in dialogue and action

- **Asylum and refugee issues**

We provide an independent Jewish voice in matters of public policy relating to racial equality and social justice.

We work closely with individuals from different communities and a wide range of organisations.

Our resources are highly valued by people both inside and outside the Jewish community. The resouces and programmes provided by JCORE complement the National Curriculum and the Foundation Stage Curriculum.

JCORE provides INSET on race equality education and the implementation and monitoring of race equality policies. We provide assemblies and workshops and can recommend resources, supply speakers and offer support with curriculum development.

Foreword

"As a South African who was forced to go into exile in the 1960s and as a Jewish woman, I am delighted to see that JCORE has produced this informative and practical book filled with ideas, advice and resources for introducing an awareness of race equality issues at a fundamental stage of teaching and learning. 'Start with a Difference' allows children from a variety of settings to actively learn about living in peace and celebrating the similarities and differences that exist between people. It is an excellent two-pronged approach. It enables teachers and support staff to recognise and accept their own and other's individual differences and to help children understand, respect and enjoy the diverse world in which they are growing up.
As the Co-coordinator of Persona Doll Training, I am delighted to see this book acknowledging the role that Persona Dolls can play in promoting equality and justice and in challenging racism and other social inequalities.

"Start with a Difference" will appeal to everyone who believes that the differences between us are an asset to be enjoyed, valued and celebrated."

Babette Brown
Co-ordinator of Persona Doll Training

Further copies available from:

JCORE
PO Box 47864
London, NW11 1AB
Tel: 020 8455 0896
Fax: 020 8458 4700

admin@jcore.org.uk
www.jcore.org.uk

Registered Charity Number: 281236

First published March 2006
© Jewish Council For Racial Equality
ISBN 13: 978-0-9552745-0-3
ISBN 10: 0-9552745-0-8
All rights, reserved. Material may be photocopied for private, non-profit making educational purposes only

Start With a Difference
Promoting Race Equality in the Early Years

A Jewish Perspective

Contents

- **An introduction to race equality** 1
    - Why 'Start with a Difference'?
    - What is inclusion?
    - Ofsted
    - Promoting race equality in the early years
    - What is a race equality policy?
    - What is race equality education?
    - What is multicultural education?
    - What is anti-racist education?
    - Involving parents
    - Curriculum guidance for the Foundation Stage
    - Checklist
    - Developing the global dimension

- **Resourcing a culturally diverse setting** ..15
    - Resources for an early years setting
    - The home corner
    - Persona dolls

- **Myself and others** 27
    - Activities
    - Three bears project
    - Using books

- **My family** 37
    - Activities
    - Books and resources
    - Celebrations, special days and events
    - Festival websites
    - Festival books
    - A calendar of festivals and special days

- **My home** 49
    - Activities
    - Books and resources

- **Journeys** 57
    - Activities
    - Books and resources

- **Food** 65
    - Activities
    - Books and resources
    - Using bread as a theme

- **Light and Colour** 73
    - Activities
    - Books and resources
    - Colour poems

- **Using books to promote race equality and global citizenship** 81
    - A Triangle for Adaora by Ifeoma Onyefolu
    - A Balloon for Grandad by Nigel Gray & Jane Ray
    - But Martin by June Counsel
    - Elmer by David McKee
    - Emeka's Gift by Ifeoma Onyefolu
    - Handa's Hen by Eileen Browne

- **Rhymes songs and poems** 97

- **Resources** 107

- **From policy to practice** 115
    - Race equality policy template
    - Race equality audit

An Introduction to Race Equality

An introduction to race equality

- To prepare children for life in multicultural Britain.

- To provide children (particularly in predominantly white settings) with the resources, activities and discussion that represent the diversity of society.

- To begin the long term process of raising awareness of the issues around race equality and multicultural education.

- To provide a hands-on practical guide for early years educators which will encourage the implementation of race equality in their setting.

- To provide a publication integral to the implementation of race equality policies.

- To fulfil the requirements of the Foundation Stage curriculum which refer to multicultural and race equality education.

- To allow children to develop a growing awareness of, and a positive commitment to understanding their responsibilities as Jews to make the world a better place.

Start with a Difference does not intend to teach about other faiths and festivals. There are many resources available that can provide this. Start with a Difference offers an approach to learning where race equality permeates the curriculum and becomes a natural part of the ethos of the setting. It describes how a setting can provide an environment that enables children to learn about themselves and others in a positive way, allowing them to see their place both in their community and the wider society. The book is intended for use in both Jewish and non-Jewish settings and is inspired by values which are common, human principles.

Why start with a difference?

> If we begin with our children and our grandchildren then we just might live to see a community and nation and world which respects and celebrates diversity, a world in which we all live together without prejudice, discrimination and hate
>
> Institute of Citizenship

This book makes an important contribution to the education of young children for many reasons. **The Jewish Council for Racial Equality** has already published **Let's Make a Difference** for primary schools and **Making a Difference** for secondary schools. **Start with a Difference** completes the sequence (sometimes described as the most important age) and offers a vital starting point for educators providing race equality education.

This book offers guidance for teachers on how to give children a sense of who they are and how their family, their home, their educational setting and other aspects of their lives all contribute to their identity. They also need to understand the notion of community, their place in it, how their school or nursery is a part of a community and how the Jewish community is part of a larger community. This will apply equally to other faiths and cultures that constitute society. We need to see our place in this ever-increasing community. Whilst we need to have a strong sense of our own identity, we also must understand that we are surrounded by diversity and that we must learn to appreciate, understand and equally respect those in the wider society. It is fundamental that our children are educated to understand that human beings share a common humanity and are all of equal worth.

> Work for peace within your household,
> then in your street, then in your town
>
> Bershibber Rabbi (Eastern Europe)

Judaism's message of social justice should be planted at an early age and continued throughout the children's education. Jewish people have a moral responsibility to respect and care for each other and for those in the wider society. Jewish tradition teaches us to "Love thy neighbour as thyself." (Leviticus 19:18). These are also basic principles of the personal, social and emotional curriculum at the Foundation Stage.

Young children need to develop a strong sense of identity but are still able understand their similarities to and differences from others as a natural part of the learning process. All settings, whatever their location, cultural/ethnic composition should ensure that the children are provided with opportunities to respect and value similarities and differences equally. The plurality of the Jewish world provides a starting point for looking at our connections with others. Just looking at a small group of young Jewish children may provide us with children from Ashkenazi (descendants of Jews from Germany, Poland, Austria and Eastern Europe) and Sephardi (descendants from Spain, Portugal and North Africa) backgrounds. There are often bilingual children and children who have moved from one country to another. It is important that we integrate this learning into the curriculum and build upon the children's own experiences.

Jewish settings similar to all white or mainly white settings have a particular challenge. As there are fewer representatives of society at large, there is a need to work harder at presenting images of others in a positive way, without being tokenistic or presenting stereotypes. The principles, however, remain the same. The children need to be surrounded by images of different people through the resources that they are presented with, the stories they are read and the discussions that the children engage with.

Basic Jewish principles teach us to be tolerant, understanding and respectful and to strive to make the world a better place. Educators have a responsibility to provide a curriculum that promotes these essential principles. The race equality dimension should be a natural part of the planning process and an essential component of an inclusive setting.

What is inclusion?

Inclusion forms an integral part of race equality education. Inclusion is a fundamental principle in the government initiative, 'Every Child Matters'. The aim of inclusion is to embrace all people, taking positive account of race, gender, disability, medical or other need. It is about giving equal access and opportunities and eliminating discrimination and intolerance. Inclusion means that educational settings must adapt to the needs of the every child, working towards providing effective planning in order to meet individual needs.

Inclusion is about providing equal opportunities for all children in a warm, welcoming and relaxed environment which promotes respect and tolerance. This means promoting the development of all children and ensuring that they and their families feel included and valued, in an atmosphere which encourages an appreciation and understanding of diversity.

The term inclusion applies to diversity in its broadest sense, embracing all groups (whether they are part of the setting or not) who may be disadvantaged or marginalized. The National Early Childhood Forum describes inclusion as "A process of identifying, understanding and breaking down barriers to participation and understanding" and describes **"a sense of belonging as the best indicator of inclusion."**

Ofsted

Ofsted guidance for early years settings states that staff should, "Actively promote equality of opportunity and anti-discriminatory practice for all children." Inspectors base their judgements on the extent to which:

- All children are included and their differences acknowledged and valued.
- All children have access to appropriate toys, learning resources and equipment.
- Resources are used which reflect positive images of culture, ethnicity, gender and disability.
- The needs of all children are met.

Children need to feel valued and be free from discrimination. When staff are committed to equality they recognize that children's attitudes towards others are established in the early years. They understand relevant legislation and plan to help children learn about equality and justice through their play. The provision is carefully organised and monitored to ensure all children have access to the full range of activities. Family members and staff work together to share information about cultures, home languages, play activities and children's specific needs.

Ofsted: Sessional day care: Guidance to the National Standards

Promoting race equality in early years

Background to the law

The Race Relations (Amendment) Act 2000 strengthened the Race Relations Act 1976. It came about as a result of the Macpherson Report into the murder of the Black teenager, Stephen Lawrence (pictured left). The Race Relations (Amendment) Act 2000 obliges or places a statutory duty on public authorities and maintained early years settings to: 'eliminate unlawful racial discrimination and promote equality of opportunity and good relations between persons of different racial groups'.

Developing & monitoring race equality

The Race Relations (Amendment) Act 2000 requires early years settings supported by Public Authorities (including nurseries, nursery schools, children's centres, neighbourhood nurseries and early excellence centres) to have a race equality policy which is essentially a three-year strategy and action plan that states how the public authority will implement the policy. Voluntary, independent and private early years and childcare settings and services do not have the same statutory duty as public authorities. It is, however, good practice for all settings to be guided by the principles of equality and justice which underpin the law.

This statutory public duty means that there is no choice about complying; it applies to all public authorities whatever their minority ethnic population. The publication **Learning for All** produced by the Commission for Racial Equality highlights the standards that schools and early years settings should aim to achieve to encourage inclusion and promote race equality.

It is important to recognise and accept that the need to eliminate unlawful racial discrimination and promote equality of opportunity applies equally in all settings, whether rural, suburban or urban. This is as important where children are from one racial group as it is in multiracial and multicultural settings. Aspects of the policy will differ greatly from one setting to another. The emphasis will be quite different in an inner London nursery compared with a synagogue nursery.

It is our duty as early years educators to prepare our children for life in a diverse society. A comprehensive race equality policy provides a strategic approach, enabling short and long-term objectives to be realistic and effective. Staff need to think carefully about the practical implications when implementing the policy, ensuring that all are striving towards the same goals and creating an ethos that promotes race equality.

Adults working in early years settings need to be fully aware of how discrimination in all its forms can affect the development of children. Guidelines and strategies to counteract discrimination must be developed, implemented and monitored.

Unless ways of countering the negative effects of discrimination on pupils and their families in early years settings are devised, development may be limited from the outset of the children's education.

Adapted from Sure Start: Promoting Race Equality in the Early Years
by Jane Lane (Policy director, Early Years Equality)

What is a race equality policy?

The race equality policy should be a working document which highlights the principles of race equality within the setting, describing the setting and what it is offering in terms of promoting race equality. Targets for improving race equality should be set and the policy should be monitored and regularly reviewed. The template in this book (see *From Policy to Practice* page 116) offers a useful starting point from the perspective of a Jewish or other setting.

Another useful starting point is the completion of the race equality audit form (see *From Policy to Practice* page 118). This will highlight the areas that should be addressed by the setting and will contribute to the targets. Local authorities Sure Start programmes provide race equality training courses and there are many helpful books and documents available (see *resources section* page 107). This book will be helpful in terms of the implementation of the policy. It offers practical ways of providing a culturally diverse environment and activities which complement the curriculum and topics taught at Foundation Stage.

What is race equality education?

Race equality is described by Robin Richardson[1] both as a 'measurable outcome' and as a 'moral value or principle'. Race equality is what we should be striving to achieve in our settings – a recognition of diversity and equality. It is about eradicating racism and valuing diversity. As early years practitioners, we have a particular responsibility to counteract the negative effects of discrimination on pupils and their families and to challenge and prevent racism.

Children usually reflect the racial attitudes in their personal environments. Unless their educational environment is positive towards difference, it is likely that they will hold those racially prejudiced attitudes that are prevalent in our society which will have been formed prior to their learning in an early years' setting.

It is also necessary to adopt an anti-racist approach that incorporates multicultural education or 'multiculturalism' and anti-discriminatory practices, to ensure that all forms of stereotyping, prejudice and discrimination and all forms of racism are identified, examined and understood. One component without the other will not provide children with the tools necessary to develop the skills and knowledge required or provide the curriculum and ethos necessary to promote race equality.

What is multicultural education?

Multicultural education emphasises the celebration of cultural and religious differences. This provides an education aimed at preparing children to live in a multicultural society by giving them an understanding of the culture and history of different ethnic groups. Examples include: organising activities, visitors, visits, cultural events and exchanges to increase understanding and appreciation of a variety of cultures, for example, cookery, music, dance and storytelling. This provides an opportunity for children to experience aspects of other cultures or religions and may increase children's ability to value their own culture as well as those of others.

Multicultural education must also include the various cultures of white people. Understanding other cultures and religions should help to prevent the ignorance that leads to stereotyping and racism. However, whilst a multicultural approach emphasises cultural and religious differences, it may ignore and obscure issues of racism and the promotion of race equality. It can be tokenistic and may reinforce existing prejudices based on stereotypical representations of other cultures, religions or lifestyles. A narrow multicultural curriculum focusing on exotic culture does not create an atmosphere of respect. A snapshot of other cultures could actually be more damaging than doing nothing at all. The promotion of cultural diversity, religious tolerance and understanding is insufficient alone but valuable when presented within an anti-racist framework.

What is anti-racist education?

Anti-racism has now become almost synonymous with race equality (the term more commonly used) though the emphasis is slightly different. Anti-racism describes the conscious effort that we make to challenge and combat racism in all its behavioural and institutional forms. Anti-racist education examines the wider structures within the institution, developing a policy and strategies to address institutional racism in all its forms. This will also include the curriculum, staff training, recruitment etc. which are reviewed regularly. Staff, parents and children are made aware that the school takes this issue seriously and is committed to change. Staff and governors are provided with a shared vision and strategic framework for tackling practices and procedures that may be discriminatory.

The hidden curriculum must be addressed by all members of staff. This is the environment that the children are surrounded by and the things that they learn that are not actually taught through the formal curriculum. It is the messages that they receive through the ethos of the setting, the resources, posters, displays and books. The interaction between pupils and teachers, the questioning by members of staff and others involved in the children's learning and the discussions that are encouraged all contribute to a set of value systems within the hidden curriculum. The hidden curriculum has been described as what children learn by default. If these areas are closely considered through a whole-school approach, the 'institutional body-language' of the setting is likely to reflect an environment that is both inclusive and anti-racist.

What is an anti-discriminatory approach?

> Children are not born prejudiced.
> It is something they learn.
>
> Jane Lane (Former policy director, Early Years Equality)

While eliminating racial discrimination and promoting equality of opportunity are important in ensuring race equality, they are insufficient alone in countering any prevailing attitudes and behaviour. We need to adopt an approach that counters any negative attitudes and behaviour that children may have already learned. As early years educators our responsibility to do so is crucial. Evidence shows that dormant (and not so dormant) racist attitudes are widespread before children are four years old and that some children actually become aware of cultural, racial, gender and class differences from the age of two.[2] Babies are not born prejudiced. As they grow, they acquire their attitudes from everything that surrounds them; books, toys, the media, friends, family, teachers, carers, what they see (or don't see), what they do and what is said (and unsaid). Children develop their self-identity and attitudes towards others and make judgements about those differences.[3]

Early years educators have a responsibility to ensure that children learn positive values and attitudes. They must address issues relating to diversity and equality and ensure that the children with whom they work are provided with opportunities to learn to respect difference. The children should grow to reflect the attitudes of their environment. They need to learn positive attitudes to difference in skin colour, culture, religion and language, using sensitive methods taught in positive and constructive ways. Educators in a mono-cultural setting have a specific role to play, presenting positive images of diversity as the children may not have encountered other cultures or religions previously. The role of parents cannot be underestimated. They should be familiar with the policy, work towards its aims, and share and own the policy, helping to build an ethos that promotes mutual respect. It is essential that we involve families in the learning process, as they are often the key influences in children's lives. Embedding anti-racism and multiculturalism into the nursery or school ethos gives all children the opportunity to develop their potential and allows racist attitudes and practices to be challenged.

Early childhood is not the time of innocence so very often described. Children are born innocent, without prejudices, but exposure to the people and images that surround them soon contribute to build up their picture of the world. All of their early experiences play a part in the construction of attitudes and impressions. Children become aware of cultural, racial, gender, class and physical differences from a very early age.[4] They begin to develop their self-identity and attitudes towards others and will have learned positive and negative feelings about racial groups, often by the age of two.[5] The setting therefore plays an important part in the development of young children's identities and their attitudes towards others.

Involving parents

Parents/carers new to the setting should receive a copy of the setting's equal opportunities policy and race equality policy. This will help parents to understand the values of the setting and the staff's expectations of the children and their families. When meetings are held with parents/carers they should be shown resources and staff should explain why they value resources from other cultures and why everyday images of minority ethnic people are important for a child's development. Inclusive and multicultural displays also provide evidence about the values of the setting.

Parents/carers should feel wanted, valued and involved. They have a positive role in the setting which should be encouraged. Their linguistic, cultural and religious backgrounds should be seen as an asset to the setting and parents should be invited to demonstrate and participate in activities.

Communication between parents/carers and the setting should be regular and the setting should be willing to share information about the child and show a willingness to work together with parents/carers. Staff should make time to listen to parents/carers and use the time at the start of the day to have exchanges with parents.

The setting has, "a commitment to the child within the family as well as to the child as an individual. Supporting and working with families is seen as a vital part of a child's development and well being."[6]

Adapted from EYTARN 1998 (Early Years Trainers Anti-Racist Network)

Curriculum guidance - Foundation Stage

(Curriculum Guidance for the Foundation Stage – QCA 2000)

The basic principles for early years education emphasise the importance of inclusion. Children should all feel included, secure and valued. Parents and practitioners should work closely together, supporting each individual child and ensuring that no child is disadvantaged. A positive attitude to learning should be encouraged, through rich and stimulating experiences. The displays and equipment surrounding the children should reflect the community that the children come from and the wider world and the environment should be free from stereotypical images and discriminatory practices.

The six areas of learning recognise the part that race equality plays across the curriculum. The **Personal, social and emotional development** and **Knowledge and understanding of the world** make direct reference to issues relating to race equality whilst the areas, **Mathematical development**, **Creative development** and **Physical development** can link with activities which might encompass race equality more indirectly. **Communication, language and literacy** will be an integral part in the development of race equality across the whole curriculum.

Personal, social and emotional development

- Understand that people have different needs, views, cultures and beliefs that need to be treated with respect.

- Understand that they can expect others to treat their needs, views, cultures and beliefs with respect.

- Encourage children to talk with each other about similarities and differences in their experiences and the reasons for those similarities and differences.

Knowledge and understanding of the world

- Find out about past and present events in their own lives and the lives of their families and other people they know.

- Begin to know about their own culture and those of other people.

- Look at books that show a variety of languages, dress, customs.

- Deepen children's knowledge of cultures and beliefs, e.g. looking at books, listening to stories in different languages, handling artefacts, inviting visitors to the setting from a range of religious and ethnic groups and visiting local places of worship.

---

1 Robin Richardson (2003) *Removing the Barriers to Race equality Education – Steps for Promoting Race Equality in Education*

2 Louise Derman Sparks (1989) *Anti-Bias Curriculum: Tools for Empowering Young Children*, Washington DC: National Association for the Education of Young Children

3 Jane Lane (2001) *Dealing with Prejudice and Discrimination: the issues. Practical Pre-School* (Issue 25) Leamington Spa: Step Forward Learning,
Jane Lane (1999) *Rights and Wrongs*, Nursery World, London, TSL Education Ltd

4 J.E. Maxime (1991) *Towards a Transcultural Approach to Working with Under Sevens*, Early years Anti-Racist Network, National Children's Bureau

5 David Milner (1983) *Children and Race: 10 years on, London*: Ward Lock Educational

6 Iram Siraj-Blaatchford (1994) *The Early Years – Laying the Foundations for Racial Equality*, Stoke-On-Trent: Trentham Books

Developing the Global Dimension in the Foundation Stage Curriculum

The curriculum is increasingly teaching children to learn about themselves as members of a community, to take responsibility for themselves and for others and to recognise that they also belong to a much wider community. They are developing a greater awareness of other people, places and cultures and the similarities and differences between people. The global dimension shares many common characteristics with the race equality dimension.

"In the Foundation Stage children are offered a variety of experiences that encourage and support them to begin to make connections between different parts of their life experience. They become aware of their relationships to others and the different communities that they are part of, for example, family and school. They begin to develop awareness of diversity of peoples, places, cultures, languages and religions. They begin to understand fairness, the need to care for people and the environment, and to be sensitive to the needs and views of others."
(DfES Developing the Global Dimension in the School Curriculum – March 2005)

The themes of this book focus on the child's immediate environment – family, school and community, their way of life and their experiences. These can be directly compared and contrasted to people in this country or around the world. In this way you can move children on from the known to the unknown, valuing their identity but also exploring how they relate to the wider world.

Personal, social & emotional

- Children consider people in particular situations and whether they might be happy, sad, hungry or lonely using pictures or photographs.

- Children look at photos of other children from around the world and discuss what needs we all have such as love, a home, friends, food, water, security and shelter.

- Children listen to and discuss stories from different countries about issues of right and wrong, the needs of others and how we can help one another.

- Children talk about places they have visited for different reasons, for example on holiday, for recreation, religion or to visit relatives. They discuss how they feel about places.

- Practitioners encourage children to try activities from different cultures and contrast similarities and differences for example, food choices relating to cultural and religious traditions.

Communication, language & literacy

- Children listen to and talk about stories from around the world.

- Children imitate the positive, anti-discriminatory language of the practitioner.

- Children hear a range of languages. Community languages are valued. Children are introduced to a range of written scripts and dual-language books.

Knowledge & understanding of the world

- Children explore photographs, books and artefacts from around the world and reflect on similarities and differences between people and places locally and elsewhere in the world, Children are introduced to a range of cultures and religions through stories, music, dance, food and role-play using clothes, cooking implements, symbols and toys.

- When looking at distant 'strangers' in photographs or video, children can be encouraged to imagine ways of life based on common or familiar experiences: food, brothers and sisters, toys and games. In other words, similarities can be emphasised as well as differences.

- Children take part in role play (such as being a travel agent) to explore what different places are like, using brochures, pictures and children's own holiday photographs. Locate these places on maps.

Physical development

- Children play games and learn dances from diverse cultures which show interdependence and promote cooperation.

- Children shop for, prepare and taste food and discuss what it is like and where it is from.

Creative development

- Children participate in music, dance and games from different places. Parents/carers are encouraged to share their own songs and artefacts.

- Children use patterns, textiles and designs from diverse cultures and countries.

Mathematical knowledge

- When discussing numbers, children's experience of number in a range of languages is shared with others.

- Children play counting games from different countries and count objects from around the world.

- Children look at photographs/drawings showing how a range of cultures use number, shape and pattern.

(Taken from DfES Developing the Global Dimension in the School Curriculum – March 2005)

Checklist for race equality education in an Early Years setting

- ✓ Examine current policies, practices and procedures and assess whether race equality is being promoted in all areas.
- ✓ Ensure that racism is challenged at all levels.
- ✓ Include the contributions of all the children in our settings.
- ✓ Value the contributions to society made by different ethnic groups and individuals.
- ✓ Encourage children to develop positive attitudes about others.
- ✓ Encourage empathy and understanding.
- ✓ Integrate children's stories of their everyday life into their learning.
- ✓ Encourage children to think critically, to consider different perspectives, to analyse information and make up their own minds.
- ✓ Promote equality of opportunity – ensure that all children in the setting are equally valued, treated with equal concern and that the needs of each are addressed.
- ✓ Explore with children that no one culture, language or religion is superior to another.
- ✓ Provide resources, for example, books, music, art and display that reflect the lifestyle, culture and traditions of the widest possible range of communities, demonstrating a commitment to cultural diversity.
- ✓ Be aware that practitioners are an important factor in the lives of children. Interaction between children and practitioner plays a crucial role in the educational process.
- ✓ Provide an environment which promotes mutual respect, open-mindedness and a range of teaching styles which enable children to have an active role in their own learning.
- ✓ Provide children with an understanding of how their setting is a community that constitutes an important place in the wider community.
- ✓ Create an ethos of acceptance, inclusion and recognition of diversity.
- ✓ Raise awareness of the need to assess our own attitudes, prejudices and opinions about different ethnic and cultural groups.

Jewish Settings

- ✓ Jewish values are used to teach children about others.
- ✓ Help children to understand what their responsibilities are as Jews in the building of a more just society.

Resourcing a culturally diverse setting

Resourcing a culturally diverse setting

It is essential that all children have access to positive images with which they can identify. They also need to be surrounded by positive images reflecting the wider society which are not necessarily represented in the setting. The resources make a valuable contribution towards the ethos of the setting and provide children with an environment which creates a natural part of their learning.

- Welcome posters, reflecting the children in the setting, children in Britain and the world
- Global photo collections – calendars, postcards, magazines, world map, globe
- Festival boxes containing artefacts and pictures for each festival celebrated
- Photo albums – of nursery children in different contexts – trips, activities, play etc.
- Posters – portraying people, festivals and other cultural events
- Photographs of different children and families in the UK and around the world
- Writing area – different languages on the wall or writing table covered with different scripts, numerals, laminated alphabets available for children to look at or copy
- Images displayed from the local environment, local shops, buildings, street signs which reflect the local and wider community
- Photographs of the children, their self-portraits and drawings
- Numbers and words translated into different languages on displays
- Materials – from African Caribbean, South American, South Asian shops to hang on walls, Musical instruments from around the world
- Multicultural resources – puzzles, games, dolls etc.
- Book corner – posters and variety of multicultural books, dual language books, Hebrew books
- Hello, goodbye and welcome in different languages
- Quotes which illustrate the ethos of the setting
- Variety of artefacts from other cultures
- Musical instruments from around the world
- Links to the wider community

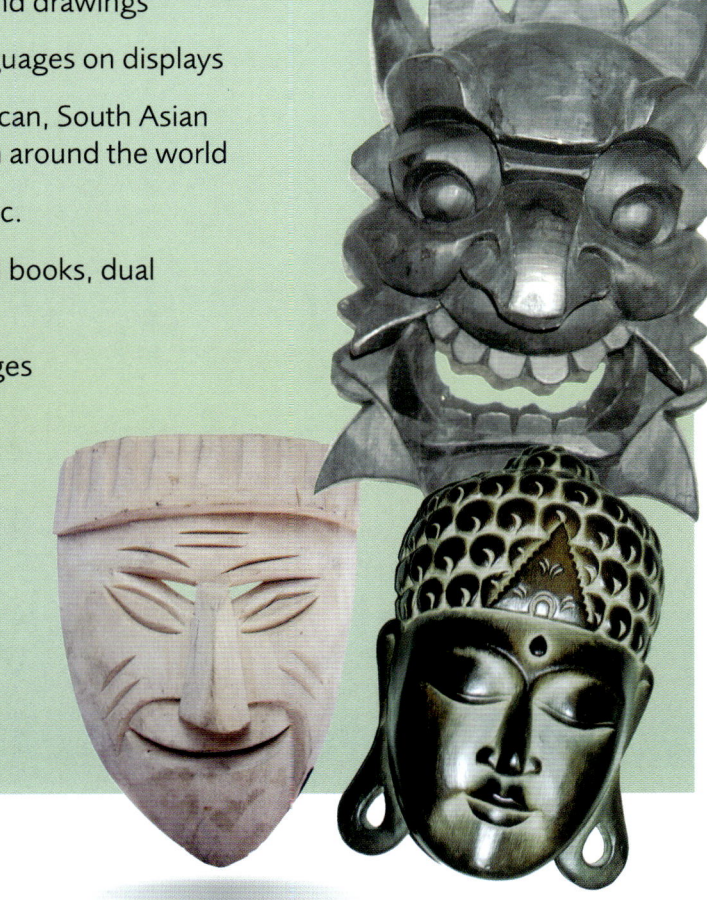

Resources for an early years setting

ARTEFACTS

> Artefacts are interesting and enjoyable to work with and can help to bring cultures alive. They stimulate pupils' curiosity, discussion, creativity and powers of observation and detection. They help children realise the limits of their understanding, as well as encouraging their research skills in finding out more.
>
> Oxfam – Global Citizenship

Whether artefacts are brought back from holiday, have a particular religious or historical significance or are handcrafted, they can really capture children's interest. Young children love to bring in their own artefacts and see other peoples'. They should be allowed to touch, hold and closely examine artefacts that we show them or that individuals bring in to share.

Where to find artefacts of interest?

- Visiting Chinese and Asian supermarkets to buy different foods or kitchenware.
- Visit charity shops, particularly in areas that are culturally diverse.
- Talk to parents - have they any artefacts which they can share, or would like to bring in and talk about or donate to the setting.
- Bring artefacts from other countries.
- Musical instruments from other countries.

GLOBES AND MAPS

Children as young as three can be introduced to maps and globes which can be used very simply. They will be able to identify the land and the sea and we can show them Britain. They will also be keen to find countries where relatives may live. They can then see the rest of the world in relation to the UK. A map of the world should be on permanent display so that children can make the link between themselves and the places that you are discussing. A playcloth world map is a useful resource that children can sit round on the floor. Providing children with maps to look at will help to develop children's spatial skills and their knowledge and understanding of the world. When using maps, talk to the children about where they have been and whether it was a long or short journey and how they travelled there. This will help to enhance their understanding.

Photographs and pictures

The images that we present to children are as important as the words we say to them. Images should represent the setting but should also reflect the diversity of the UK and the wider world. Children should look for both similarities and differences in images and always find the similarities first, however small. It's also important to establish the commonalities of people and their experiences before looking for the differences. It is important that children see examples of poverty and affluence, men and women and rural and urban settings. Children should be encouraged to bring in pictures of their own to show and discuss. It is important to select images carefully, avoiding stereotypes, though children will often perceive an image in a certain way which may need to be countered through questioning and discussion. A range of different photographs will help to ensure that people and places are represented in a balanced way.

Questions to ask about images:

- Where was the image taken?
- Which people are in the image?
- What are they doing?
- What are they saying to each other?
- What is different?
- What are they wearing?
- What in the picture is similar to you and your life?
- How do you think they are feeling?
- What objects are in the image, and what are they for?
- What is the environment like?
- What might happen next?
- How does the image make you feel?
- Are there any problems in the image, and what action could be taken to tackle them?

Images can be easily downloaded from the following websites:

www.oxfam.org.uk/coolplanet/teachers/photopps/gallery.htm
www.google.co.uk (click on 'images')
www.freefoto.com
www.sln.org.uk/geography/Images.htm
www.sln.org.uk/wow/
www.landsat.org (for a satellite image gallery)
www.globaleye.org.uk ('On Camera' section for images of the developing world)
www.earthfromtheair.com (for a collection of aerial photographs)
www.geographyphotos.com (images for teaching geography)
(QCA innovating geography)

Activities using images

- Cut a picture into six pieces. Talk to the children about each part as they put it back together.
- Ask children to give photographs a title or a caption.
- Give a child (or group) a photograph. Ask them to tell you what they can see and you draw the picture on a large sheet of paper or a whiteboard.
- Cut out part of a photograph. Talk about the part that is left and then ask the children what else may be in the rest of the picture that they can't see. After the discussion, add the missing part of the photograph.

Toys and games

- Look for resources when your are on holiday. Bring a children's book home showing that country's language, or visit a toy shop and bring home an authentic toy.
- Supplement your toys with small world people reflecting different backgrounds.
- Use games from around the world particularly in outdoor play.
- See list of suppliers of multicultural toys (*Resource section* page 107).

Music and songs

- Have on display a selection of musical instruments from around the world. Include objects such as a shofar (the ram's horn which is blown on Rosh Hashanah – Jewish New Year)
- Make musical instruments with the children such as shakers, tic-tac drums and rainsticks.
- Have collections of music from different cultures available.
- Invite musicians representing different musical traditions e.g. African drumming. (*Resource section* page 107)

Books and stories

- Counting books from around the world
- Dual-language books
- Multicultural books
- Non-fiction books about others (*Using books* page 81)

Visits, trips and community links

Every setting will have access to its own wealth of people with their rich personalities, experiences and lives. The use of people and visits can provide a valuable way of extending children's knowledge and understanding of the world. First hand resources are more exciting and effective as tools for children's learning.

- Visit local place of worship
- Look at different types of restaurants
- Visit a supermarket
- Visit a travel agent
- Visit local shops particularly shops selling different foods

The Home Corner

> The home corner should be a changing and stimulating area for play which reflects our multicultural society.
>
> The Early Years – Laying the foundations for Racial Equality
> Iram Siraj-Blatchford

In order to promote anti-racist values, children need to be surrounded by resources from a variety of cultural contexts which encourage and promote cultural diversity and challenge stereotypes. Enhancing children's understanding of how others live, both in the UK and around the world, through role play will help them to see the similarities and differences and will prevent prejudices from forming.

Examples of ideas for the home corner or role-play area:

- Everyday artefacts which promote cultural diversity
- Photo albums showing families from different ethnic backgrounds, celebrating festivals and other cultural events
- Wall hangings and pictures
- Baskets
- Variety of plastic fruits and vegetables
- Lanterns
- Decorative material from Asian, South American, African-Caribbean shops used to decorate tables or as cushion covers
- Greeting cards in different languages, displaying different people
- Kitchen utensils – 'thava' for chappati making, thali bowls, Chinese rice bowls, woks, chopsticks, plastic containers with different pulses, spices etc.
- Home corner recipes books from around the world, different types of breads – matzah, challah bread, pitta bread, chappatis, popodams
- Dressing up clothes – everyday costumes for both sexes, including a range of jewellery and scarves
- A range of authentic looking black dolls from different ethnic groups with a range of clothes
- You could set up the home corner as a home from a different country or culture using objects from daily life or use a story as a stimulus for role-play, creating an area where children can role-play scenes from the story using artefacts

Persona dolls

Persona dolls are an exciting and innovative addition to any early years setting. They can be used to explore a wide range of issues and are an effective and fun way to counter discrimination and raise equality issues with young children.

The dolls are about 84 centimetres tall and look very life-like. They are beautifully dressed in quality shoes and made-to-measure clothes. There are representatives from many religions and cultures, for example a Sikh boy, a Muslim girl wearing a shalwar kameez, a Chinese boy and girl and a variety of African-Caribbean children. There are also dual heritage dolls and a doll in a wheelchair. They are dolls with their own personalities, life histories and likes and dislikes and they are small friends to whom the children can relate. They have families, go to nursery or school and they have personalities which develop over time. They are a powerful tool for exploring issues of racism, gender, disability, health, culture, religious and other equality issues through storytelling sessions. There are strong links between Persona dolls and the principles and practices underpinning the Early Learning goals.

The dolls and the stories they tell provide an interesting way to combat prejudiced attitudes and to develop respect, compassion and understanding for others. They help children to express their feelings and ideas, think critically, challenge unfair treatment and develop empathy with people who are different from themselves. The storytelling sessions boost the self esteem and confidence of the children and also offer them the support, skills and strategies they need to deal with discrimination and exclusion.

Why use Persona dolls?

- A doll's persona can be created. This allows them to be used for any situation.
- They can reflect the children they are working with in terms of age, sex, race and cultural background, and also reflect children who are not present, e.g. those with disability or those from a different culture.
- They introduce children to social diversity, enabling children to learn about the richness and variety of different lifestyles.
- They are friends that can assist children in developing strategies for dealing with unfairness against themselves and others and value positive experiences.
- They encourage children to see the similarities and differences between the dolls and themselves which will help to break down barriers.
- They help children to develop empathy and understanding which may make them less likely to feel inferior or superior to others and more likely to develop responsible social attitudes.
- They enable children to see their own individuality and life experiences valued, building up their self-esteem.
- They help children to develop non-discriminatory attitudes and understanding and to equally value each other.
- They capture the imagination of pupils and help them help develop vocabulary and oral skills.
- At the Foundation stage the dolls help develop skills, knowledge and attitudes that the children need to achieve the Early Learning Goals.

Objectives when using Persona dolls

- To encourage children to learn about different lifestyles and so introduce social diversity.
- To present positive images of Black children and their families.
- To help children gain an awareness and understanding of the richness and variety of different lifestyles.
- To make the different backgrounds of the children visible to others in the group.
- To enable children to discover what they have in common with those from different ethnic backgrounds.
- To provide opportunities for children to see their own individuality and life experiences valued, thereby building self-esteem.
- To enable children to identify with and relate to the personality created through the doll.
- To help develop non-discriminatory attitudes and understandings amongst the children.
- To tackle issues (such as name calling or rejection of a pupil) which have arisen in the school or setting.
- To encourage the children to consider the feelings of others, empathise and give advice, without personalising the situation.
- To help children learn self-help strategies for dealing with perceived unfairness.
- To challenge the stereotypes and prejudices that underpin racism and other social inequalities.

Examples of stories (Milton Keynes EMASS) (Persona Dolls in Action)

- Kofu is upset because Mark and Kate won't let him play football with them at playtime.
- Julissa is excited because she is going to visit her family in London at the weekend.
- Sally is going to be a bridesmaid when her mother gets married at the weekend.
- Eleanor loves playing with Samuel's train set and her friend laughs at her because she thinks girls shouldn't play with trains.
- Shanti says that Ahmed is a girl because he cried when he had his vaccination.
- Rose and Akua are angry because someone has just called Mohammed a racist name in the playground.
- One of the teachers has shortened Adamu's name to Adam. He can't decide how he feels about this.
- Fatima is nervous about going swimming because she will have to take her glasses off.
- Gita will be celebrating Diwali tomorrow and she is really looking forward to it.

Children's dispositions and attitudes

Nyla is upset today because she wanted to join in the group playing with the new tea set in the home corner. She sat on the rug, watching all the children setting out the cups and saucers. She felt very sad because she longed to go to the tea-party, but she was worried that someone would say that she couldn't play.

- Have you ever felt like this?
- What made you feel better?
- How can we help Nyla?
- What would you do if Nyla came to join you playing with the tea set?

Children's self-confidence and self-esteem

Peter is worried because every time he plays in the sand, some children take the sand toys away from him. He doesn't know how to stop it happening. Now he doesn't go to play in the sand unless there's nobody else there.

- Has this happened to you?
- How did you feel?
- How can we help Peter?

Sense of Community

Tasneem is puzzled because it will soon be Eid and there's going to be a big party at her house. Lots of her aunties, uncles and cousins will be there and there will be presents, cards and some lovely food. Tasneem has a beautiful new dress to wear for the party. She will have to miss nursery for this party and when she tells her friends about this, they don't believe her and they say they've never heard of Eid.

- Have you been to a party of any kind?
- Did you tell your friends about it?
- How can we share Tazneen's excitement

For further information:
Persona Dolls in Action –
Support book and video
www.persona-doll-training.org

Combating Discrimination: Persona Dolls in Action – Babette Brown, Trentham Books

The Little Book of Persona Dolls –
Marilyn Bowles, Featherstone Publications
www.featherstone.uk

Myself and others

Myself & others

When teaching Foundation Stage children about 'Myself', the opportunity arises to extend this to learning about others. By engaging in such discussions and activities, the children are strengthening their own identities, yet learning about and valuing others. Children enjoy talking about themselves and their lives and within every setting there will be enough similarities and differences between the children to promote thoughtful discussion. This can then be broadened into discussions about different kinds of children that are not represented in the setting.

Celebrating diversity within an inclusive framework will provide children with an enriching environment that values and acknowledges difference. Practitioners need to spend time discussing with the children their similarities and differences and use books, creative work and circle time to stimulate discussion and enhance the children's understanding of one another. We should be projecting positive images of *all* people and teaching children to see difference as something positive which leads to understanding and respect.

Aims

- To understand, identify and respect the differences and similarities between people.

- To develop self-awareness, positive self-esteem and confidence.

- To learn to respect the differences between people in the class.

- To show respect for people's cultures by listening to what they say and by making positive statements about their views and perspectives.

- To know that there are similarities and differences between people and to develop an understanding that difference does not mean better or worse (the differences include gender, language, appearance, ability, family structure and cultural background).

- To understand the similarities and differences between children in the UK and other parts of the world.

ACTIVITIES IN THIS SECTION RELATE TO ALL AREAS OF LEARNING:

1,2,3...

Teach pupils to count to three in another language spoken by the pupils. Practise the words by throwing a beanbag around the circle and asking the catcher to repeat one, two and three, or a word in the new language, before throwing the beanbag to someone else. (Global Citizenship: The Handbook of Primary Teaching – Oxfam)

Self portraits

Children can mix paints to create the colour that is the shade of their skin. Compare portraits with friends. Discuss similarities and differences.

Self portrait masks

Use paper plates or modroc to create self portraits. Mix paints to create skin colour and use wool for hair. Display the masks with 'hello' or 'welcome' in different languages around them.

Hands

The children sit in a circle. They all put their hands in the circle and discuss size and skin colour.

Life in a Purple World

Talk to the children about the positive role that diversity plays in our lives. Tell the children this story about a world where everyone was the same. The story can be extended.

"In Purple World, everyone was the same. There was only one colour, purple, so everything you saw was purple. There was only one kind of food, purple soup, and everybody ate the soup at the same time. There were no boys or girls, just purple people who all looked the same. They all went to a purple building on purple day and they all said the same prayers and sang the same songs."

The children can then talk about how the people in Purple World might feel. After the discussion, they can look around the room and celebrate the differences they see among their classmates.

The children can then complete the statement, 'I'm different because...'

(QCA: Respect For All)

Statements

The teacher calls out questions to group the
children in different ways. For example:

Whoever has lived here all their lives come into the middle of the circle and join hands.
Whoever speaks... (choose language), come into the middle of the circle and count to five.
Whoever has family in another country come into the middle of the circle and "post" a letter to a relative.

The final statement could be one that everyone has in common such as:

Whoever is in _____ nursery come into the middle and shout "We are!".

Or

All the children sit in a circle. Ask them to change places if...

they are wearing white socks	they speak... (choose language)
they have black hair	they go to _____ nursery
they like mangos	

You may also use statements such as: 'Change places if you feel hurt if someone makes fun of you'.
Talk to the children about how it is wrong to tease someone if they are different.
Discuss strategies to combat this sort of prejudice.

or look at needs. If you need...

a home	drink	garden
a family food	crisps	love

Talk to the children
about common needs.

I like you because...

In a circle ask the children to face a partner. Each partner tells the other something that they really like about them. This could be physical features or something about their character or talents, for example, Jason says that "Sherray has beautiful plaits in her hair" or Abdul says "Samuel is very good at counting backwards."

Different lives

Show children photographs of different people – different communities, different parts of the world, different religions. Discuss what may be different in their lives. Read to the children books such as **Shompa Lives in India** by Jean Harrison or **Wake up World** by Beatrice Hollyer. Ask children to compare a day in their life to these children.

Common tastes

Go round the circle saying for example, "I like drawing and so does David." Throw the ball to David. David then chooses something that he has in common with someone else and throws the ball to them and so on.

Knock Knock at the door

The children sit in a circle. Three children are chosen to sit in the middle of the circle. The children all say ' Who's that, knocking at the door, who are they looking for?' The teacher answers the children with a question about the three children, for example, 'Someone who has blonde hair.' The children put up their hands and guess which child is being described. If the child chosen is correct, that child changes place with the child in the middle and the children all call out the new child's name in unison.

Pictograms

Create pictograms about different physical features (hair colour, skin colour, eye colour) or hobbies, countries that our families come from, number of people in family.

Hands holding hands

Cut out shapes of the children's hands. Mix paints to create the appropriate colour to paint the hands. Display the hands in a circle to demonstrate unity.

Clothes from around the world

Look at different clothes from around the world: Japanese, Indian, Chinese, Pakistani etc. Look at fabrics and styles. Make a display. Get children to create their own fabrics on paper, using printing techniques. Cut into dress shape or sari etc. and add a face.

Celebrate our differences

Use a book such as **All the Colours of the Earth** by Sheila Hamanaka or **All Kinds of People** by Emma Damon as a stimulus for creating a wall hanging of all the children's heads and shoulders in the setting. Use skin tone fabric. This could be stuffed to give a more three-dimensional effect. Use wool, plaited or scrunched or with beads, curly dolls hair (available from craft shops). Use fabric pens, different materials and buttons for clothes.

Make a 'dream quilt'

Tell the children the story of Martin Luther King and how he dreamed of a world where people didn't fight and hate each other because their skin colour was different. Give each child a hexagon shape cut out of white card. Talk to them about what a quilt is and how they can make a quilt by joining all the hexagons together. Ask the children to draw a picture of themselves. Stick all the hexagons together to make the quilt which illustrates the similarities and differences in your setting.

New child

Use dolls, puppets or Persona dolls to introduce somebody different to the children as part of a circle time activity. Present the doll with a character. Then let the children ask questions and present the children with a scenario to discuss.

Hands & feet

Look carefully at the children's handprints and footprints. Compare with each other. Order from smallest to biggest.

Silhouettes

Draw outlines of some of the children. Paint or use collage to decorate. Talk about differences and similarities.

Fingerprints

Talk to the children about fingerprints and how each of them are unique. Show examples of fingerprints blown up. Children can create patterns using their fingerprints with an ink pad. Create a display with photos, fingerprints and self-portraits which identify each child's individuality. You may include a quote from each child, "I like..."

Poetry

Write poems together on the themes of similarities and differences. Introduce the word 'unique'. Use a framework such as:

I have brown hair
Yours is black
I have blue eyes
Yours are brown
I like skipping
You like to swim
And we both like chocolate
Yum, yum, yum

'What's in the box?'

Glue a mirror to the bottom of a box. Tell the children that there is something very special in the box and that there is only one like it in the world. Ask the children what they think it is. Pass it round a circle or get the children to come and look at it one by one and tell them not to tell anybody what they saw in the box. When all the children have looked, ask them what they saw in the box. Talk to them about how everybody is unique and special in their own way.

Shades of Black

Read the story **Shades of Black** to the children. Ask the children to describe their hair, skin or any other feature in a similar way for example, "My hair is thick and golden like a lion's mane."

Three Bears project

Use the story of The *Three Bears* as a project about another kind of family. There are many opportunities here to discuss similarities and differences and to encourage the development of language.

- Ask the children to bring in their favourite teddy bear. Discuss similarities and differences in terms of colour, size, feel of fur etc. Find the biggest, smallest, cuddliest, tallest, shortest. Children talk about their own bears and that each is unique and special – appreciating and valuing all bears. Take photographs of all the children with their bears.

- Circle games. 'If your bear is a big bear, change places...' 'If your bear is cuddly change places' 'If your bear likes honey...'

- Circle time. Use a bear to discuss any issues that arise in the setting, for example, the bear may be sad because another bear would not let her play in the home corner.

- Set up the three bears house in the home corner with bear hats. Provide bowls, spoons, a cot, small mattresses, Ready Break and milk so that the children can try to make the porridge. They can also tidy up. Children will realise that only four people can play and that they must take turns.

- Make porridge. Try it with honey, raisins, sugar, salt. Discuss taste and texture.

- Make a bears' cave, den or forest where the bears can all be kept.

- Use the story **Whatever Next** and create a role play area based on the story. Provide the children with a box, a colander, wellies, a toy owl, a picnic basket. Put a moon on the wall and make a chimney.

- Discuss the moral aspects of the story. Was Goldilocks right or wrong? How did Goldilocks feel? How did the bears feel?

- Ask the children to re-tell the story. Record the children's stories on tape.

- Take photos of play in the bear house and photos of the children with their bears.

- Maths activities. Ordering the size of the bears and bowls. Count the bears. Count how many small bears, big bears etc.

- Paintings of the children's bears.

- Cook different-sized bear biscuits.

- **Bear rhymes:** 'Bears bang with 1 hammer...'
  'Ten bears in the bed'
  'When Goldilocks went to the house of the bears'
  'Ten brown teddies'

- Organise a teddy bears picnic. Children to take their bears to a park for a picnic. Make cakes.

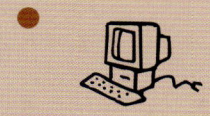

- Teddy's Day Out. Teddy visits different places of worship and looks for symbols that he might find. Teddy Bears Picnic – Sherston CD ROM
  http://www.leicester.gov.uk/education/learninglibrary/ks1/re/teddys_day_out/index.htm

- **Books**
  Teddy Bears Picnic – Mark Burgess
  Teddy Time – Mark Burgess
  One Little Teddy – Mark Burgess

- Take a the nursery bear home for a visit. Pack a suitcase. Parents fill in a d ary describing bear's activities.

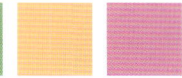

Using books

Using books to teach about similarities and differences

The list below includes just some of the wonderful books which highlight the similarities and differences between people. The questioning and discussion leading from these stories should be carefully thought through as there are many possibilities for extending children's learning. Many of the activities in this section can be used with these stories and there are also opportunities for work across the Foundation Stage Curriculum. These books are also appropriate for older children.

All Kinds of People – Emma Damon
All Kinds of Bodies – Emma Damon
Why Noah Chose the Dove – Eric Carle
All the Colours of the Earth – Sheila Hamanaka
The Fire Children – Eric Maddern
Two Eyes, a Nose and a Mouth – Robert Grobel Intrater
The Sneetches – Dr Seuss
Shades of Black – Sandra L Pinkney
I Love My Hair – Natasha Tarpley
My Nose, Your Nose – Melanie Walsh
My World, Your World – Melanie Walsh
You're all Animals – Nicholas Allan

Elmer – David McKee
The Rainbow Children
Long Blue Blazer – S Willis
Something Else – Kathryn Cave
But Martin – June Counsel
Cleversticks – Bernard Ashley
Am I Really Different? – Evelien Van Dort
Just a Little Different – Mercer Mayer
Children Just Like Me – Anabel Kindersley, Barnabas Kindersley

(see resource sections for publ shers)

My Family

My family

☀ Personal, social & emotional

- **Discuss the meaning of family:** What does family mean? Who is close family? Why is my family so special? Ask children to bring in photographs of their family. Talk to them about members of their family and draw pictures of them. Who lives in your house? Who has family that lives in another country? Ask parents to tell children about different members of the family and any family in other countries. They may also wish to share memories of family members who have died. (N.B. It is important that practitioners are aware of and sensitive to complex family situations.)

- **Prayer:** Is prayer important in your family? How often do you pray? Who prays? Where do we pray? Consider the fact that many children do not pray. Talk to the children about how people pray in different ways and in different places and that prayer is universal. What do we need to pray? Talk about the special book and other practices associated with prayer. Look at artefacts used by different faiths. Talk about different places of worship. (virtual synagogue and mosque, **www.hitchams.suffolk.sch.uk/synagogue/index.htm**).

- **Respect for family and others:** Discuss the meaning of respect. Why should we respect our family? What is respect? Why is it so important? Who else does this extend to? Respect at school, respect within the community and the wider community. Talk to the children about respecting differences. What happens if we do not respect people's differences? (Story: **Frog in Winter**)

- **How are families different?** What makes a family? Look at pictures of different types of families. Ask children to bring in pictures of their families to talk about. Some children will have some family in this country, some in other countries. Why is that? How many generations can they count in their families? Use photopacks to look at pictures of families in the UK and in different parts of the world. How are they similar and different? Emphasise the similarities before looking at differences.

- **Special family occasions:** Invite families to come and talk about special celebrations. Bring in artefacts, clothes, gifts and food. Children can talk about their experiences and ask questions. Make a display using artefacts and photographs.

- **Grandparents – why are they so special?**
Have a grandparents open afternoon.
Invite grandparents to come in and tell stories
about their lives and their families.

- **Names:** Talk about names. Ask children to find out where their names come from. They may have been named after someone in their family. Why was that person special? If not, why was their name chosen? Why is a name so important? Discuss middle names, nick-names, names for grandparents, such as nana, granny, oma, opa, saba, and others.

Communication, language & literacy

- **Story: Emeka's Gift** (*Using Books* page 92) Emeka searches for a gift for her grandmother.

- **Story: A Balloon for Grandad** (*Using Books* page 86) Abdulla's balloon floats away, perhaps to grandad in another country.

- **Family and artefacts:** Ask children and families to bring in artefacts that they can talk about such as artefacts used for prayer. Children may bring in a tallit (prayer shawl), a kippah (head covering), a siddur (prayer book), a Muslim prayer cap, a Muslim prayer mat, a rosary. Look at similarities and differences between prayer caps.

- **Celebration role-play:** Use dressing up clothes to encourage children to role-play a celebration in their family. Provide artefacts to encourage the children to use their knowledge and experience. Children may use this opportunity to order events, for example, a birthday party. They may play games, make a pass-the-parcel and set the table for tea. They could celebrate Passover using artefacts such as Haggadot, wine cups, matzah and matzah cloth. Children may dress ready for the Seder (special meal) and use these artefacts to re-enact a Seder.

Knowledge & understanding of the world

- **Where is your family from?** Ask parents and the children to find out where their families are from. Look at a world map and a globe and try to locate these places. Mark on the map where families come from. Talk to the children about people moving and why they may go to live in other countries. Ask children to bring in photographs of family in other parts of the world.

- **Other families:** Look at photographs of other families in the UK and in different parts of the world. Discuss similarities and differences. Look at clothes, family members and celebrations.

- **Events and celebrations in families:** Birthdays, Christenings, baby blessings, Bar/Bat Mitzvah, weddings, births and naming ceremonies. Give children the opportunities to talk about their family celebrations and encourage children to role-play special family ocassions and celebrations.

Creative development

- **Family tree:** Give each child a tree shape to paint. Stick photos of their close family, names or drawings on the tree. Talk about a family tree. Involve parents.

- **Peepo house:** Make a Peepo house with lift-the-flap windows. Children draw or stick photographs of each member of their family in the windows. Decorate the houses.

- **Wishing tree:** Create a wishing tree/wall - the children draw a wish for a member of their family.

- **Family books:** Make books about families. Draw pictures, stick photographs, write names. Involve parents.

- **Weddings:** Talk about wedding customs in different cultures. Ask children to talk about weddings that they have been to. Were they bridesmaids or a page-boys? Look at books and photographs that show different types of weddings. Children bring in photographs or other souvenirs to share. Have a wedding in the nursery. Make invitations, dress children up, play music and eat.

- **Family portraits:** Children paint portraits of members of their family. Display the portraits with children's descriptions of the person and names in different languages (e.g. ima - Hebrew, mama - French)

Mathematical knowledge

- **How big is your family?** Talk to the children about the size of their families. How many people live in your house? How many siblings? Create a pictogram. Children stick on numbers. Who has the biggest/smallest family? Some children may have extended family living in their homes and may wish to include them. How many sisters and brothers do your parents have?

- **Family Order:** Talk about who is the oldest and youngest in the family. Order family members from the oldest to the youngest. Talk about ordinal numbers.

Physical development

- **Role-play:** Use the story **Emeka's Gift** (*Using Books* page 92) to act out the different parts of the story and the journey that Emeka makes to visit his grandmother.

- **Photo frame:** Make a wooden frame for a family photograph. Paint and decorate the frame and ask the children to bring in a photograph to place inside.

- **Candle-holders:** Make different types of candle holders using salt dough or clay. Decorate when dry. These can be adapted for different purposes – Shabbat candle, diwas for Diwali, chanukiahs.

Jewish themes

- **Family celebrations:** Weddings, Bar/Bat Mitzvah, festivals, Shabbat, baby blessings.
- **Synagogue:** Talk to the children about when they go to synagogue and why. What do they enjoy at synagogue? Look at the website showing a virtual synagogue (see Personal, Social & Emotional section).
- **Prayer:** Look at the different artefacts used for prayer – tallit (prayer shawl), siddur (prayer book), kippah (head covering), wine cup and candles. You may wish to compare these with other faiths.
- **Derech eretz**: Talk about the concept of 'Derech Eretz' - small acts of kindness and 'Chessed' – loving kindness. Talk about the sedra 'Chayei Sara' where Rivka learns 'chessed'. She collects water for Avraham's servant, Eliezer, and for all of his camels in the desert sun. (Bereishit 24; 18-20)

Books and resources

NON-FICTION

Paul Mason	**Weddings**, Heinemann, 2003
Isabelle Monk	**Family**, Carolrhoda Books, 2005
Angela Wood	**Homing in: A Practical Guide for Religious Education**, Trentham Books, 1998
Emma Damon	**All Kinds of Beliefs**, Tango Books, 2000
Gwenyth Swain	**Celebrating**, Milet Publishing Ltd, 2004
Margy Burns-Knight	**Welcoming Babies**, Atlantic Books, 1997

FICTION

Jill Paton-Walsh	**When Grandma Came**, Puffin Books, 1993
Jill Paton-Walsh	**When I was Little Just Like You**, Puffin Books, 1998
Helen E Buckley	**Grandmother and I**, Sagebrush, 1994
Helen E Buckley	**Grandfather and I**, Sagebrush, 1994
Ifeoma Onyefolu	**Emeka's Gift**, Frances Lincoln, 1998
Debbie Bailey	**Families**, Annick Press Ltd, 1999
Susan Varley	**Badger's Parting Gifts**, Harper Trophy, 1984
Valerie Flournoy	**The Patchwork Quilt**, Puffin Books, 1995
Ifeoma Onyefolu	**Here Comes Our Bride!: An African Wedding Story**, Frances Lincoln, 2004

POSTER PACKS

Families themes box - Hope Early Years catalogue www.hope-education.co.uk
Families poster pack - Hope Early Years catalogue www.hope-education.co.uk
Posters ('Family and I' and 'Generations II') available from www.multicultural-art.co.uk
Families Pack – Save the Children 2002
Big Family Packs – Action Aid
Family Album (set of 32 colour photos of families within the UK) – Oxfam

Celebrations, Special Days & Events

Celebrations are extremely important to young children and will be remembered by them as momentous occasions when families and friends get together. Children should be given the opportunity to talk about the occasions they celebrate and to share with others the artefacts, food and photographs that form part of their particular festivities.

The diagram on page 47 shows the different types of events and festivals that children may celebrate. These will include religious festivals and cultural events as well as personal achievements. Through school and nursery, children will also be encouraged to take part in special days and events such as Black History Month and Refugee Week.

It is important to value and praise children's achievements as well as to celebrate the festivals and events that are important to them. This will help to raise self-esteem which is vital in fostering positive attitudes and developing respect for others.

The outer circle on the diagram (Festivals) gives examples of other festivals that the children may learn about or be aware of but may not necessarily celebrate. In a Jewish setting children will spend a significant amount of time learning about Jewish festivals. There will also be opportunities to mention other celebrations and make connections. There are many similarities between festivals celebrated by different religions that young children will be able to appreciate, for example Chanukah and Diwali. Both are festivals of light, both share themes of good and evil and both involve the lighting of candles.

The uniqueness of the traditions of religious festivals play a significant role in the development of children's identities, but it is also important to consider the universal, wider aspects that are being taught. Festivals should also be helping children to develop respect and empathy and consideration for others. Children celebrate festivals in different ways, often in a non-religious or secular way which should also be respected.

Home-school scrapbook

A home-school scrapbook encourages children to collect family photographs, memories, writing and other memorabilia from both home and school which can be brought to school and shared with the other children or taken home to be shared with families. Parents should be encouraged to help their children make contributions to the scrapbooks. This provides an on-going record of events and experiences in the children's lives. The scrapbook could be shared at a certain time each week.

The calendar on page 46 contains festivals celebrated by Hindu, Muslim, Christian, Sikh, Jewish, Chinese, Buddhist and Rastafarian people. It also contains special days, some of which relate to global citizenship. The dates of some festivals vary from year to year as some communities use a lunar calendar. The website **www.support4learning.org.uk/religious_calendars/index.cfm** will tell you the exact date of the festivals. The websites below will provide more information about celebrations.

Web sites

www.tts-shopping.com
Religion in Evidence – artefacts, books etc. on all major world religions

www.topmarks.co.uk/ChineseNewYear/ChineseNewYear.aspx
Facts about Chinese New Year

www.pbskids.org/sagwa/games/countdown/index.html
Games and stories about Chinese New Year

www.infantsreonline.org.uk/festivals_options.php
Christmas and Easter interactive stories

www.ngfl.northumberland.gov.uk/Christmas/nativity/nativity.html
Build your own Nativity scene

www.underfives.co.uk/
Ideas for all major festivals

www.ngfl-cymru.org.uk/vtc/ngfl-flash/wedding/wedding.html
An interactive site with activities and information about Christian weddings

www.woodlandgrange.leics.sch.uk/iwb/RE/harvest%20book.swf
An interactive book about harvest festival

www.primaryresources.co.uk/re/re.htm
On-line activities and powerpoint presentations on different festivals

www.knowledgehound.com/topics/holidays.htm
An A-Z of most festivals and celebrations with links to other websites

Books

Nasreen Akhtar	**Samira's Eid**, Mantra Publishing, 2000
Chris Deshpande	**Celebrations: Diwali**, A&C Black, 1994
Jo Ely	**Festivals – Big Book**, Pelican, 1998
Sue Fitzjohn, Minda Weston	**Festivals Together: A Guide to - Multicultural Celebration**, Hawthorn Press, 1993
Anita Ganeri	**The First Book of Festivals**, Evans Brothers, 2005
Lynne Hannigan	**Sam's Passover**, A&C Black, 1994
Monica Hughes	**My First Festivals** – set of 8 (inc. My Christmas, My Diwali, My Rosh Hashanah, My Baisakhi), Heinemann, 2003
Dilip Kadodwal	**Holi: The Hindu Festival of colours**, Evans Brothers, 1998
Lynn Huggins-Cooper	**Festivals: A First Look at how People Celebrate Around The World**, Hodder Wayland, 2004
Katy Jones, Linda Mort	**A Child's Eye View of Festivals** – video and resource book, SCM Canterbury Press, 2005
Grace Lin	**Kite Flying**, Dragonfly Books 2004
Saviour Pirotta, Sheila Moxley	**Joy to the World: Christmas Stories from around the Globe**, Frances Lincoln, 2000
Jillian Powell	**Why is this Day Special? A Birthday**, Franklin Watts Ltd, 2005
Jillian Powell	**Why is this Day Special? A New Baby**, Franklin Watts Ltd, 2005
Jillian Powell	**Why is this Day Special? A Wedding**, Franklin Watts Ltd, 2005
Sylvia A Rouss	**Sammy the Spider's First Hannukah**, Kar-Ben Copies Inc, 1993
Sylvia A Rouss	**Sammy the Spider's First Passover**, Kar-Ben Copies Inc, 1998
Sylvia A Rouss	**Sammy the Spider's First Sukkot**, Kar-Ben Copies Inc, 2004
Linda Smith	**Dat's New Year**, A&C Black, 1994
Kate Tucker	**Foundations: Celebrations** – Book and CD, Scholastic, 2004
Anne Witherington	**Food for Festivals – Big Book**, Pelican 1998
Jonny Zucker	Jewish Fesivals – Set of 4
	Eight candles to Light: A Chanukah Story, Frances Lincoln, 2005
	It's Party Time: A Purim Story, Frances Lincoln, 2005
	Four Special Questions: A Passover Story, Frances Lincoln, 2005
	Apples and Honey: A Rosh Hashanah story, Frances Lincoln, 2005

A calendar of festivals & special days

January	Martin Luther King Day	**Chinese** New Year	**Sikh** Birthday of Guru Gobind Singh		
February	**Islamic** Al Hijra New Year	**Islamic** Eid-ul-Adha	**Christian** Candlemas Day	**Jewish** Tu B'Shvat	
March	**Hindu** Holi	**Jewish** Purim	**Sikh** Sikh New Year	World Water Day	Red Nose Day
April	**Jewish** Passover	**Christian** Easter	**Sikh** Baisakhi	**Chinese** Ching Ming	
May	**Buddhist** Wesak	**Buddhist** Buddha's Birthday			
June	**Jewish** Shavuot	**Chinese** Dragon Boat Festival	World Refugee Day	World Environment Day	
July					
August	**Hindu** Raksha Bandhan				
September	**Jewish** Rosh Hashanah New Year / **Jewish** Yom Kippur	**Chinese** Chinese Moon festival	**Jewish** Succot / **Jewish** Simchat Torah	International Day of Peace	**Rastafarian** Rastafarian New Year
October	**Muslim** Ramadan	**Hindu** Diwali	Black History Month	World Food Day	One World Week
November	**Muslim** Eid-ul-Fitr	**Sikh** Birthday of Guru Nanak	International Children's Day		
December	**Jewish** Chanukah	Human Rights Day	**Christian** Christmas	**Chinese** Chinese Harvest festival	

SPECIAL DAYS/WEEKS
(SEE CALENDAR FOR DATES)

FESTIVALS

FAMILY CELEBRATIONS

PERSONAL CELEBRATIONS

BIRTHDAYS
ACHIEVEMENTS
(CERTIFICATES, BADGES, STICKERS)
NAME DAYS

BIRTHS
BABY BLESSINGS/NAMING

CEREMONIES

WEDDINGS

BAR/BAT-MITZVAH

SHABBAT
VISITING SYNAGOGUE OR OTHER PLACES OF WORSHIP

WORLD BOOK WEEK

WORLD WATER DAY

HARVEST FESTIVALS

FESTIVALS OF LIGHT

NEW YEAR

FESTIVALS OF FREEDOM AND REMEMBRANCE

INTERNATIONAL DAY OF PEACE

WORLD ENVIRONMENT DAY

REFUGEE WEEK

BLACK HISTORY MONTH

My home

My home

> Let your house be open wide
>
> Ethics of the Fathers 1:5

Personal, social & emotional

- **What makes a home?** Ask the children what makes a home. Introduce the word 'shelter'. What makes a home more than a shelter? Ask the children to describe their homes. Talk about why home is a special place. What makes our homes so special? What do we like about other people's homes? What do we not like?

- **People in my home**: Ask the children to describe all the people that live in their homes. Talk to the children about the common need for shelter, security and love. Talk about children's rights and the fact that for some children these basic needs are not met. N.B. Home for some children may not represent safety and security. We must be sensitive to this.

- **Homes in the UK:** Ask the children to describe different kinds of homes in the UK, for example, flats, bungalows, hostels, farms and different types of houses. How can we tell the differences between old houses and new houses? What are the differences? What might it be like to live on a farm, or at the top of a block of flats? (Use **All Kinds of Homes** by Emma Damon)

- **Homelessness:** Talk to the children about people who have no home, and about traveller and gypsy communities. Ask them what it might feel like to have no home or to move around from place to place.

- **Refugees:** Discuss with the children the fact that some people are forced to leave their homes because of war or natural disasters.

- **Moving house:** Ask the children if anyone has ever moved house. What was the reason? How did it feel? Some children may have moved from a different country. Why do people move from one country to another?

- **My Home:** Ask children to close their eyes and think about the place in which they live. Ask them to share with the group what they saw. Did they picture their house, their road, their garden, their local area? Talk about how the place we live can mean different things to different people. Encourage children to talk about their homes in relation to the local community. What do they like about the place they live in? What do they like about the people that live nearby? Show the children a simple map of the area with landmarks. Do friends live near them? Do they walk home together or walk past their homes? A large map or an interactive whiteboard would allow children to show their street and other familiar places.

Communication, language & literacy

- **Different kinds of homes:** Take a walk around the local area and look at different types of homes. Take photographs and discuss with the children. Talk about the different shapes, sizes and features of the buildings. Show children pictures of other homes that they may not be so familiar with, for example, flats, bungalows, detached houses, terraced houses and farms. Look for similarities and differences. Ask the children if they would like to live in these types of homes. Why? Why not? Use **All Kinds of Homes** by Emma Damon.

- **Books about homes: A Pig is Moving In** describes a non-stereotypical pig in his new home. **Rosie and Jim** live on a barge, **Handa's Hen** shows pictures of a home in rural Kenya.

- **This is our House:** Use the story **This is our House** by Michael Rosen. Use this book for circle time to discuss how it feels to be left out. This may lead to a discussion about being different and how children can all get along together. Discuss how the children play in the home corner and welcome others to join them.

Knowledge & understanding of the world

- **Homes in other countries:** Use **All Kinds of Homes** by Emma Damon. Children need to understand that people living in rural places live very differently from those living in cities. Try to relate this to where the children live and consider the similarities and differences. Show children pictures and discuss. N.B. It is important when looking at different homes to emphasise that not everybody in that country lives like this, particularly when looking at homes in African countries.

- **Visit to a building site:** Introduce children to the materials that are used to build a house and talk about the fact that a building is not stable enough without foundations.

- **Front doors:** Talk to the children about 'front doors'. What number is their door? What colour? What is it made of? Does it have glass on it? What else is found on a front door? Encourage the children to talk about the letterbox, the key hole(s) and handles. Ask the children to paint their front door. It may be useful to take the children for a walk around the area to look at different kinds of doors.

Creative development

- **Preparing for special occasions:** Encourage the children to tidy the home corner and prepare for a special occasion. Provide play tool kits for DIY in the home corner. Prepare the home for a special family celebration.

- **Through the window:** Ask the children what they can see through a window in their house. Provide them with a cut-out window frame and ask them to draw what they can see. Display the window frames with speech bubbles saying 'I can see…' Label some of the features.

- **Model homes:** Make model homes from junk materials. Provide children with corrugated paper, card and shiny paper or coloured cellophane for windows and doors. Make houses from duplo, megablocks and other construction materials. Ask the children to talk about their buildings.

- **My house:** Ask children to bring in a photograph of their home or send a disposable camera home with the children. Ask them to do a drawing of their house next to it. Bring in pictures of other kinds of homes found in the UK such as blocks of flats, terraced houses, detached houses, mobile homes, traveller and gypsy homes.

- **A 'different' home corner:** Make the home corner into a home from another culture or country.

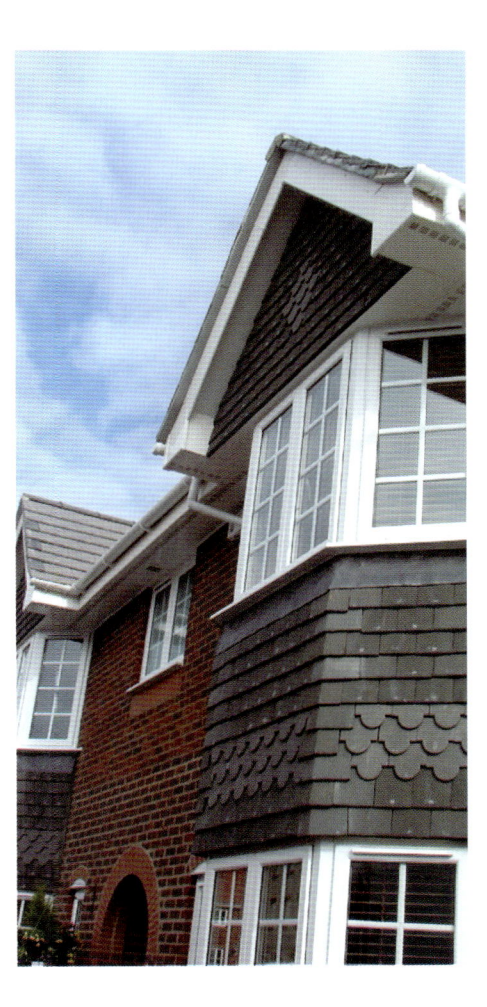

Mathematical knowledge

$1+3=4$
$2+8=10$

- **How many?** Count objects at home, the number of rooms, windows, doors and stairs. Talk about house numbers. Give children plastic numbers. Can they make their house number?

- **Dolls' house:** Sort the furniture in a dolls' house. Where do the different objects belong. Use positional language, for example, 'under', 'next to', 'on' 'near'.

- **Problem solving:** Use different types of blocks to build with. Count them. Make a tower with 6 blocks. Make a tower with 10 blocks. Which is taller? Shorter?

Physical development

- **Build a home:** Provide the children with different types of materials, such as, blankets, bricks, sticks, chairs and boxes. The children can create their own home or den. Ask them to describe the structure and how they made it. What can they use it for?

- **Moving around the home:** How do you move around the home? Think about activities in different rooms. Which rooms are calm – for sitting or lying down? How do you move up or down the stairs. What do you do in the garden? Running? Climbing? Jumping? Skipping? Ask children to act out their movements in certain parts of the house. The other children guess where they are. How do other family members get up and down the stairs? – babies, older grandparents.

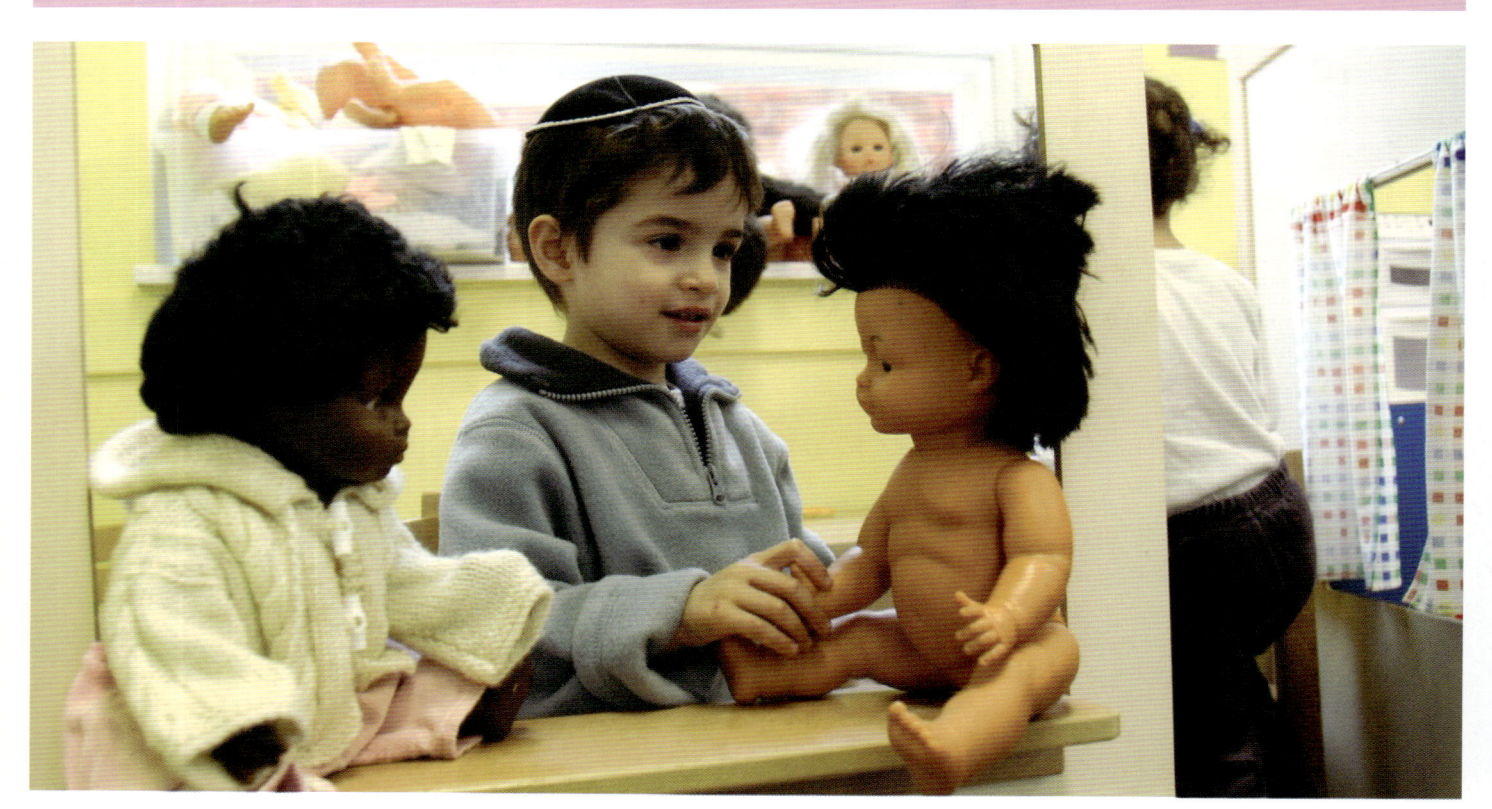

Jewish themes

- **Symbols in the home:** Discuss the meaning of symbols in the home such as mezuzah, candlesticks, challah cloth, siddur.

- **Routines at home:** Talk about routines – daily, weekly, weekends, Shabbat. Ask children to talk about the order of activities, for example, making Shabbat.

- **Hachnasat Orchim:** Talk about Hachnasat orchim – the mitzvah of hospitality. How do we make people welcome? Ask the children how they make people feel welcome in their homes. Tell the story of Avram and Sarai welcoming the strangers (messengers) in the desert (Genesis 17:1-22). Link this with welcoming customs from other cultures.

- **Make a tent:** Create a tent or use a pop-up tent with many different openings. Children can take it in turns to welcome visitors in different ways for example washing feet which happened in the Avram and Sarai story, making Rangoli pictures which Hindu families do at Diwali and making refreshments. The children can think about the needs of their visitors and use play food etc. to welcome them.

- **Homes as a Shelter:** Think about homes as shelters. This can link to Succot (Tabernacles). Talk to the children about the Israelites wandering through the desert. This also links with the idea of homelessness. Create a Succah and ask children to welcome visitors to their Succah. This could be visitors from outside the nursery for example children from another nursery or special needs school, the elderly or the lollipop person. Use a Succah for small world play and encourage children to welcome visitors to the Succah.

- **Decorate a box:** Decorate with pictures of foods and ask families to bring tins and packets of in-date food to put in the boxes for the homeless or for a refugee centre.

> You too must love the stranger,
> for you were strangers in the land of Egypt
>
> Deuteronomy 10:19

Books and resources

Non-fiction
CAFOD	**'Where is my home?'** Posters and activities
Oxfam	**Around the World:** Homes and primary topic posters: Homes
Clare Beswick	**Foundation Themes: Homes**, Scholastic, 2003
Emma Damon	**All Kinds of Homes**, Tango Books, 2005
Ann Morris	**Houses and Homes**, Mulberry Books, 1995

Fiction
Jan Ormerod	**Who's who in our street?**, Walker Books, 2000
Michael Rosen	**This is our house**, Candlewick Press, 2005

- **Map-making:** Create maps with the children of a journey they have made or make up an imaginary journey. Draw symbols representing landmarks, events, things that they see and hear. Use a book such as **We all Went on Safari** by Laurie Krebs or **Handa's Hen** by Eileen Browne and ask the children what they think they would see and hear on the journey.

- **Where in the world?** Create a display showing where the children's families originate from. Use a world map and photographs. Connect with string the photographs and places. Involve parents. (See photograph on page 62)

Creative development

- **Passports:** Make passports containing photographs of the children. These can be used for role play. Bring in examples of passports (maybe from different countries). Why do we have them? What information do they have in them?

- **Imaginary journeys:** Send the children on an imaginary journey. Introduce the idea of a magic carpet to take them to a different place in the world. Use a small rug that they can sit on in turn. Ask questions, such as, What can you see? What can you hear? What is the weather like?

- **Storytime:** Read/tell the children a story about a journey. Provide pictures or props for them to act out the story e.g. **We're going on a Bear Hunt** by Michael Rosen. You could use a story tape.

- **Footprints:** Make footprints leading to a certain place in the outdoor area. The children can explore where they lead to and use them in their imaginary play. Count the number of footprints.

- **Travel agent:** Make the home corner into a travel agents or the check-in at an airport (Resources: tickets, brochures, suitcases/bags, computer, luggage labels, timetables, maps, airmail letters, postcards – children could design their own posters of different countries)

- **Fill an empty bag:** Give the children a picture of an empty bag or suitcase. Draw or cut and stick pictures of all the things they would need if they were going away.

- **Create a journey:** Take a programmeable toy (a roamer or a pixie) on a journey. Create a journey based on a story. This could be the journey of the balloon in **A Balloon for Grandad**, Rosie's journey in **Rosie's Walk**, Handa's journey to find the hen in **Handa's Hen** or the bear hunt in **We're Going on a Bear Hunt**.

- **Journey across the world:** Use a 'playcloth' world map placed on the floor. Highlight the UK as a starting point for a journey. Children can take dolls and teddies on journeys to different parts of the world. A collection of bags and items to pack could also be available. Stick pictures on the map to help children recognise different parts of the world.

$1+3=4$
$2+8=10$

Mathematical knowledge

- **Vehicle Sorting:** Sort toy vehicles into different groupings – type, size, colour, speed.

- **Journey around the nursery:** Use a programmeable toy (Roamer or a Pixie) to create journeys around the nursery setting, for example, from the reading area to the home corner or from the climbing frame to the shed. The children can describe the route using positional language.

- **Footsteps:** Ask the children to count how many footsteps from one part of the nursery to another. Repeat the trip but use a different route. Explore the difference. Which way is the quickest? Slowest?

Physical development

- **Journey out of Egypt:** Tell the children the story of the Exodus. Use sand and small world play equipment to re-enact the story.

- **Assault Course:** Make an assault course that represents a journey from fear to safety. Use crates, chairs and bricks to make a den for the children to escape to. Use wheelbarrows, carts and rucksacks. Use climbing equipment if appropriate. Encourage children to use locational language such as under, over, around etc. to describe their journey.

- **Grandmother's footsteps:** Play the game 'Grandmother's footsteps'.

✡ Jewish themes

- **The story of Passover**

- **Noah and the ark:** Use the story **Why Noah chose the Dove** by Isaac Bashevis Singer. This story will stimulate discussion about the different characteristics of animals and people but the importance of valuing everyone. Talk to the children about the effects of floods and other natural disasters.

- **Avram's journey:** The story of **Lech Lecha**. Avram was forced to leave his native land and he didn't know where he was going. What must this have been like for him? Compare with refugees today. Why are people sometimes forced to leave their homes?

- **The wandering Jew:** Talk to the children about the Jewish people wandering through the desert for 40 years. Plant some cuttings of 'Wandering Jew' (Tradesacantia) in a pot that they have decorated. This activity would link well with Tu B'Shvat. Place a map of the world on a table with a clump of cuttings in a vase on the top, allowing them to trail over the map. Talk to the children about how Jews have wandered all over the world for many hundreds of years. Stick pictures of flags or national costumes on a display board (International Doll Museum www.home17.inet.tele.dk/ethnics/). Add postcard or photographs of different places that children have lived or visited. Talk to the children about the different customs and traditions that come from Jews having lived in different parts of the world, the different foods that we eat and the Yiddish words that we use.

Books and resources

FICTION

Eileen Browne	**Handa's Hen**, Walker Books, 2003
Eileen Browne	**Handa's Surprise**, Walker Books, 1995
Jean and Gareth Adamson	**Topsy and Tim Series**, Ladybird Books, 2003
Ifeoma Onyefolu	**Emeka's Gift**, Frances Lincoln, 1998
Ifeoma Onyefolu	**A Triangle for Adaora**, Frances Lincoln, 2001
Nigel Gray, Jane Ray	**A Balloon for Grandad**, Orchard Books, 2002
Isaac Bashevis Singer	**Why Noah Chose the Dove**, Macmillan, 1998
Verna Wilkins	**Are We There Yet?**, Tamarind Ltd, 2002
Choi Yangsook	**The Name Jar**, Dragonfly, 2003

Food

Food

Personal, social & emotional

- **Traditional foods:** Talk to the children about traditional foods. Ask them what foods they have for certain festivals or on certain days of the week. What types of foods are from their culture? Invite parents in to talk about different foods.

- **Food and the senses:** Use the senses to explore different foods. Give children a selection of exotic fruits – mango, pineapple, pawpaw, passion fruit, pomegranate. Which look nice? Not so nice? Look at the outside then the inside. Do children change their opinion of the fruit? Taste the fruit or give them juice to try. What do they think now? Talk about how the inside is always more important – of a present, of a person. Draw pictures of the fruits.

- **My favourite meal:** Ask the children to describe their favourite meal. Where does it come from? For example, spaghetti from Italy, noodles from Asia. Use a world map to locate the different countries. Draw pictures of their favourite meal on a paper plate. Display with quotes from the children.

Communication, language & literacy

- **Describe a fruit:** Pass a variety of fruits around and ask each child to think of a word to describe the fruit that they are holding, for example, heavy, light, soft, hard, smooth, rough. The children can also smell the fruit. Cut the fruit up and ask the children to describe the inside. Discuss.

- **The journey of a banana:** Talk to the children about where bananas are grown. Explain that they are grown on large farms or plantations mostly in the Caribbean. Show the children the Caribbean Islands on a world map. Discuss the fact that many Caribbean people live in Britain today. Explain to the children that bananas are green when they are picked and only become yellow later. Show them an unripe and a ripe banana.

- **Banana cake:** Make a banana cake – See recipe: **www.oxfam.org.uk/coolplanet/kidsweb/recipes/bananacake.htm** Talk to the children about the recipe and the list of ingredients. Discuss the change in the texture of the cake mixture and the cake when baked.

- **'The Very Hungry Mouse':** Make your own version of **The Very Hungry Caterpillar** using foods from different cultures or foods that they eat at home, such as different types of breads, fruits or vegetables.

Knowledge & understanding of the world

- **Where in the world?** Ask children to bring in different food labels. Find out where different foods come from. Show the children a world map and stick the labels on the different countries.

- **Food shopping:** Take a trip to a supermarket or local food store. Look at the fruits and vegetables displayed. Try to find out where they come from. Discuss with the children the fruits that have to be grown in hot countries and the fruits that can be grown in this country.

- **Food collections:** Make collections of foods, such as, Thai, Indian, and Jewish foods.

- **Planting:** Ask the children to bring in seeds or pips from different fruits and vegetables. Plant them together and see if they grow.

- **Cookery sessions:** Invite parents to the setting to make food with the children or show different foods from their culture.

Creative development

- **Fruit salad:** Make fruit salad. Use a variety of fruits to create a fruit salad with colour, texture and different tastes. Try making smoothies with different combinations of fruit.

- **Observation drawings:** Look carefully at whole fruits and cross-sections. Discuss the shapes and patterns and ask the children to draw what they see.

- **Fruit printing:** Look carefully at the insides of fruits. Use different coloured paints to create prints of the patterns.

- **New restaurant:** Change the role-play area into a restaurant, for example, Indian, Chinese, Italian. Consider the utensils, decoration, table layout and menu. Invite parents to help set up the area and to bring artefacts to make the restaurant more authentic. Make food from playdough to serve in the restaurant. Play music.

Mathematical knowledge

$1+3=4$
$2+8=10$

- **Food sorting:** Use plastic foods to sort into different groupings, for example, fruits, vegetables, breakfast foods, bread etc.

- **Numberlines:** Create a numberline using foods or breads from different cultures.

- **How heavy?** Introduce the language 'heavy' and 'light' when looking at different foods and cooking.

- **Menus:** Collect menus from different take-away restaurants. Look at the size and shape of the menu. Discuss the colour and the text. Sort the menus according to the type of food, for example, Italian. Count the menus. How many are Italian, Chinese etc.? Talk about the different types of foods. Cut out the pictures and make collages which reflect food from different cultures.

- **Fruit pictogram:** Make a pictogram of favourite fruits. Provide children with pictures of fruits to add to a chart. Count the fruits. Find which is the favourite.

Physical development

- **Let's cook!** Discuss with the children the actions that we use to prepare certain foods, for example chopping vegetables, rolling pastry, mixing a cake mixture or kneading dough. Improvise these actions with the children.

- **Kitchen utensils:** Collect and try to use different utensils, for example, different sized cutlery, baby spoons, soup spoons, chopsticks. Show the children how to use a knife and fork correctly.

- **Fruit picking:** This would link well with Shavuot, Succot or Harvest Festival. Take the children fruit picking, or to visit an allotment or garden centre. Create your own small allotment in the outdoor area.

✡ Jewish themes

- **Succot:** Link with harvest festival. Talk about harvest all over the world. Use the theme of 'World Harvest' to incorporate a global dimension.

- **Shavuot:** Make cheese cake. Talk about the significance of cheese cake and milk products at this time. This festival celebrates the harvesting of the first fruits of the season. What are the first fruits at this time of year? Discuss seasonal foods.

- **Traditional Jewish foods and their origins**: Look at recipes, make foods. Ask parents to bring in different traditional foods.

- **Tu B'Shvat:** Festival of trees. Talk about the 15 different fruits that are eaten at Tu B'Shvat, fruits that are grown in the land of Israel, such as, olives, dates, figs, pomegranates and grapes. Taste the fruits and hold a tree planting ceremony.

Books and resources

Non-Fiction

Beatrice Hollyer	**Let's Eat! Children and their Food Around the World**, Henry Holt and Co. 2004	
Judith Jones	**Knead it, Punch it, Bake it:**	
	The Ultimate Bread-making Book for Parents & Kids, Houghton Mifflin, 1998	
Ann Morris	**Bread, Bread, Bread**, William Morrow, 1995	
Oxfam	**Come and Eat with Us**, Child's Play International, 1995	
Ann Witherington	**Food for Festivals**, Longman, 1998	

Fiction

Valerie Bloom	**A Carribbean Counting Poem**, Macmillan, 1997
Eileen Browne	**Handa's Surprise**, Heinemann, 1997
Mick Manning	**Zed's Bread**, Walker, 2001
Brita Granstrom	**A Rainbow All Around Me**, Cartwheel Books, 2002
Jama Kim Pattigan	**Dumpling Soup**, Little Brown and Co, 2005
Amy Wilson Sanger	**Yum Yum Dim Sum**, Ten Speed Press, 2003

'Bread' websites

www.goodlookingcooking.co.uk/cat_bread.html
www.fabflour.co.uk/Freestyle.asp?PageID=229
Multicultural pretend and play bread set
www.brainydays.co.uk
www.open-sez-mefestivals.co.uk/flour.htm

Using BREAD as a theme

- **Which bread?** Children talk about the different breads that they eat at home. Do they have special bread for special occasions? e.g Shabbat. Do they have certain breads with certain meals or different breads in a restaurant? Ask families to bring in samples of the bread they make or eat at home. Ask parents/carers to demonstrate how to make different breads.

- **Different breads:** Show the children different types of bread such as, pitta, challah, chappati, matzoh, naan, tortilla, bagel, soda bread etc. Talk about where the breads originate from – which cultural traditions and countries. Use a world map to locate different countries. Discuss the shape, texture, smell and weight of each bread. Talk about how bread is used for different purposes – toast, sandwiches, with soup, to eat curry. Discuss the similarities and differences between breads. Discuss personal preferences.

- **Bakery:** Introduce a range of different plastic breads in the home corner and set up a bakery. Use play dough to make breads. Visit different bakeries.

- **Bread-making:** Involve parents in making breads with children or bringing them in to share. Talk about the process of baking bread. Discuss the ingredients, texture and changes from dough to cooked bread.

- **Bread Feast:** Have a bread feast. Lay a large table with all different breads for the children to try. Provide butter, jam, fillings etc. Invite parents to join the children. Take photographs and collect comments for a display.

- **Bread display:** Varnish different types of bread with PVA glue, this will preserve the bread and they can be used for display.

Light and colour

Light & colour

Personal, social & emotional

- **Colourful us:** Discuss the differences between the children in the setting. Talk about hair colour, eye colour and skin colour. Use **All Kinds of People** by Emma Damon and see – *Myself & Others* page 27.

- **Festivals of light:** Name the different festivals of light. Discuss the festivals celebrated by the children and those celebrated by others. What are the similarities and differences? Talk to the children about light being a symbol of hope.

- **Day and night:** Talk about day and night, light and shadows. Draw around shadows. Talk about the sizes and shapes of the shadows.

- **Colour mixing:** Look at paint charts and talk about shades of colours. This can be related to skin colour, hair colour and other differences between people. Children can mix paints to create different shades of colours and consider light and dark.

- **Light sources:** Ask the children to think of different examples of light sources. How did people manage before electricity was invented? Look at examples of light sources, for example fairy lights, lamps, torches, light-up toys etc.

Communication, language & literacy

- **Candle counting:** Count different collections of candles. Encourage the children to use the language 'before' 'after' 'more' and 'less'. Ask them to describe the candles, for example, 'thin, long and white' or 'fat, yellow and patterned'.

- **Light and dark vocabulary:** Brainstorm vocabulary connected with light and dark, for example, glowing, shiny, bright, dull. Find materials that reflect this vocabulary and create a display.

- **Story:** Noah and the Ark. Tell the story and explain the significance of the rainbow. Talk to the children about peace in the context of the setting, the UK and the wider world.

- **Song: Every Colour under the Sun** by Jan Holdstock (Every Colour Under the Sun, Ward Lock educational, 1983). Use the words from the song as part of a display about the children in the setting.

- **Stories:** The story of Chanukah, the stories of Diwali and Holi, the Christmas story.

Knowledge & understanding of the world

- **Light Museum:** Make a collection of lights or a 'Light museum'. Collect torches, lamps, fairy lights, candles, night-lights, a cut-out moon and a sun. Discuss them with the children. Which are natural? manufactured? religious? Create a display. Talk about the uses of candles, for example, birthdays, Shabbat, outdoor candles and memorial candles (Yahzeit).

- **Lunar calendar:** Discuss what is meant by a lunar calendar. Talk about the cycles of the moon. Which religions use a lunar calendar? Show the children shapes of the moon changing.

- **Chinese Mooncake Festival:** This is a Chinese harvest festival to celebrate the moon goddess. It takes place on the 15th day of the 8th month in the Chinese calendar when the moon is at its brightest.

- **Fabrics around the world:** Look at different fabrics from around the world. Discuss their patterns and textures. Describe the colours and look for light and dark shades of colour. Use for display or as a stimulus for creative work.

- **Sun:** Talk to the children about the sun as a form of energy and light; the fact that one sun lights and warms the world, creates the seasons and differentiates night and day. Explain dawn and dusk and sunrise and sunset.

Creative development

- **Modelling:** Make menorahs, divas and stars using self-hardening clay. Decorate.

- **Light and Dark Tent:** Create a light/dark tent. Use torches and other lights. Provide concave and convex mirrors, colour filters and allow children to play with shadows. Use the tent to display different festivals of light, for example, a Chanukah tent may contain a chanukiah, candles, posters, dreidels, wrapped-up gifts and books.

- **Rangoli mats:** Make rangoli welcome mats using powder paint or coloured rice. Talk about the idea of welcome. Why is it so important? Who do we welcome to our setting? How do we welcome visitors or new children?

- **Festivals of light:** Make paint splatter pictures for Holi, make Indian sweets, make Chinese lanterns, make a frieze based on an Islamic design, using 2D shapes stuck together. This can also be an ICT activity using an art package.

- **Use handprints to create a rainbow:** Talk to the children about different handprints – smaller, bigger, different shapes. Count how many handprints.

- **Hand-print chanukiah:** Make a chanukiah using hand prints. Children can use 4 fingers on each hand and then 2 thumbs together to create the shamash. Add yellow tissue paper flames.

1+3=4
2+8=10

Mathematical knowledge

- **Candle Sorting:** Give the children a collection of candles to sort and describe. Use birthday candles, Havdalah candle, night-lights, Shabbat candles, church candles etc. Look at the different colours, shapes, textures etc. Also look at candle holders such as divas, Shabbat candlesticks, chanukiahs and other decorative candle holders.

- **Counting Songs:** Use familiar songs with a Chanukah or Christmas theme, for example, "Eight coloured candles, shining very bright, eight coloured candles shining very bright and if one coloured candle should put out it's light, there'll be… (to the tune of "ten green bottles").

- **Counting Candles:** Ask the children to solve simple problems, for example, 'For Chanukah we light three candles today, how many more are there to light?'

Physical development

- **Festival cooking:** Make festival sweets, potato latkes and biscuits.

- **A dark, dark place:** Den play. Provide the children with different materials and textures to create their own dark place that they can light up with torches. Use boxes, sheets, bricks, tubes, chiffon and other materials.

- **Torchlight**: Explore the light when the torch is close to and far away from different objects. When is the light provided by the torch strongest? How does the torch work?

✡ Jewish themes

- **Kabbalat Shabbat:** When does Shabbat begin and end? Discuss sunrise and sunset. Why does this change through the year? Look at Shabbat candles and Havdalah candles. Why do we light Shabbat candles? How long do they burn for? Explain why the Havdalah candle is plaited. Discuss the meaning of Havdalah.

- **Chanukah candles:** How are they different from Shabbat candles? Discuss the shape, size, the number of candles and how long they burn for. Which do we light first on Shabbat? Why?

- **Yahzeit candles:** (in memory of lost relative) – Discuss why this candle burns for 24 hours.

Books and resources

NON-FICTION

Pat Brunton	**The Little Book of Light and Colour**, Featherstone Education Ltd, 2003
Nancy Luenn	**Celebrations of Light**, Simon and Schuster Inc, 1998

FICTION

Michael Rosen	**Our Eight Nights of Hanukah**, Holiday House, 2000
Roseanne Thong, Grace Lin	**Round as a Mooncake**, Chronicle Books, US, 2000
Maureen Roffey	**Noah's Ark**, Scholastic Press, 2004
Sandra L Pinkney	**A Rainbow All Around Me**, Cartwheel Books, 2002
Wendy Cooling	**All Colours of the Earth**, Frances Lincoln, 2005

Festivals of light around the world
www.everythingesl.net/lessons.light_festivals.php

I Can Sing a Rainbow

by Arthur Hamilton

Red and yellow and pink and green,
Purple and orange and blue,
I can sing a rainbow,
Sing a rainbow,
Sing a rainbow too!

Listen to your heart,
Listen to your heart,
And sing everything you feel,
I can sing a rainbow,
Sing a rainbow,
Sing a rainbow too!

Unseen Colours

by Ruth O'Connell Brown (aged 10)

I asked the child who could not see,
What all colour was like to she.
"Oh gold a thing soft, warm and kind,
While black is like a sleeping mind.
Blue is like a rushing waterfall
And pink the sound of the sweet bird's call
Now at last, now finally,
My favourite, green, the salty smell of the crashing sea."

Multi-coloured

Red is a fire burning bright,
A swan is a soft delicate white.
Blue for the sky, sea and flowers,
Grey for the gloomy Autumn showers.
Brown the colour of my outstretched hand,
Yellow the colour of soft, warm sand
Green a colour everywhere in sight,
Black is a blanket called the night.

USING BOOKS TO PROMOTE RACE EQUALITY AND GLOBAL CITIZENSHIP

Using books

Books are an invaluable tool for the teaching of issues relating to race equality, similarities and differences, stereotyping and prejudice. Very young children are able to relate to these issues, particularly in the context of a captivating story. Books should not be read to the children as a one-off, in isolation, but activities and questions for discussion should be carefully thought through. Books are responsible for shaping children's understanding of different ethnic groups, particularly if children are in a setting that is all-white or faith-based. Exposing children to a variety of literature can help them to understand the differences and similarities between people.

It is important to use books to enable children to recognise both similarities and differences. Many books about life in other countries will highlight differences, yet children should still be provided with the opportunity to look for similarities and elements that they can relate to, rather than dwelling on exotic differences alone. We must also make children aware, when reading books about African villages (e.g. **Handa's Hen** by Eileen Browne), that not all African people live like this. These books are showing only a snapshot of rural life in Kenya or Tanzania. It is too easy to reinforce these stereotypes and omit the wider learning opportunities.

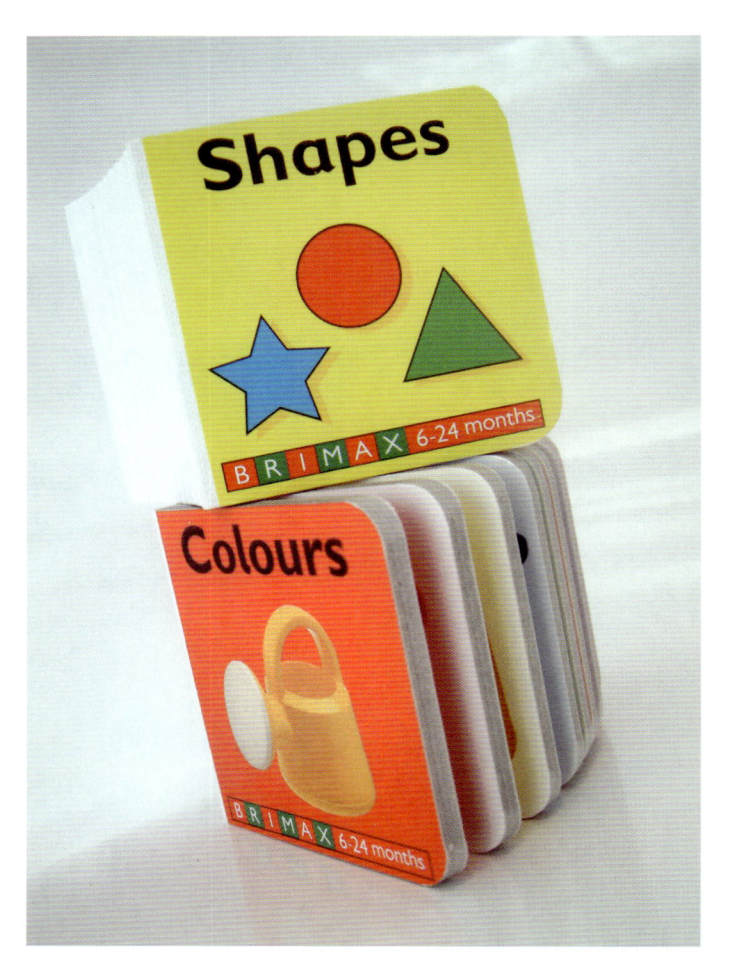

The value of books

Books:

- Develop their understanding of the lives, attitudes and perspectives of people from different cultures, races and religions.

- Enable children to learn about each other and the wider world.

- Allow children to recognise and challenge stereotypes.

- Give children the opportunity to talk about their own lives and experiences.

- Allow children to identify with the experiences and feelings that are common to all human beings and understand what makes us different.

- Allow children to empathise with characters who are treated unfairly.

- Contribute to raising the self esteem of children who can identify with characters in the books.

- Provide opportunity for texts to be followed up with constructive dialogue and questioning which develop thinking skills and avoid or counter stereotypes.

(Babette Brown – Unlearning Discrimination in the Early Years)

BOOKS IN AN EARLY YEARS SETTING SHOULD:

- Reflect a diversity of gender roles, racial and cultural backgrounds, special needs and abilities, a range of occupations, a range of ages.

- Present accurate images and information.

- Show people from all groups living their daily lives – working, with family, celebrations. Most books should be about contemporary life in the UK.

- Reflect different languages and should include alphabet books and stories in Braille.

THE FOLLOWING RANGE OF BOOKS ARE RECOMMENDED BY OFSTED:

- Books which link country and town and challenge stereotypes of farmers.
- Books which challenge stereotypes of minority ethnic groups.
- Books with traditional stories and heroes and heroines from a range of cultures including Roma and Traveller.
- Books which reflect the same story in different cultures, e.g. Cinderella.
- Texts about refugees.
- Texts which can be used to challenge racism.
- Dual language texts.

This chapter looks at a selection of books which are suitable for Foundation Stage. For each book there is a synopsis of the story, ideas for activities, questions for discussion and links to the themes covered in **Start With a Difference.**

A Triangle for Adaora — Ifeoma Onyefolu

Synopsis

Why won't Adaora eat her slice of paw-paw? She says she doesn't want to spoil the star shape in the middle - so her cousin Ugo offers to find her a triangle instead. As they walk along they see all kinds of shapes, from Uncle Eze wearing his rectangular agbada to musicians playing circle-topped elephant drums, from plants with heart-shaped leaves to a crescent-shaped plantain. And just when Adaora is too tired to look any more, they find a triangle - and a treat from Aunt Felicia! Ifeoma Onyefulu introduces children to shapes, African style, with warm words and photographs offering a colourful glimpse into Nigerian village life.

ISBN 0-7112-1467-0

Questions for discussion:

How is Adaora's life similar and different from ours? Refer to each page and discuss the pictures.

Activities:

- Find Africa on a world map/globe. Find Nigeria. Find the UK. Where are we in relation to Africa?

- Look closely at a paw-paw (papaya) fruit. Describe the outside, the inside, the star shape in the middle. Discuss the shape, colour, texture, soft, hard, heavy, light etc. Peel off the skin. What does the fruit taste like? Paw-paw trees – why are they grown in Nigeria? Talk about climate - why can't we grow them here?

- Make paw-paw and banana smoothie or sorbet.

- Search for circles, triangles, squares, diamonds, ovals, crescent and star shapes in our environment. Make a set of cards with all the different shapes and play 'snap' or 'pairs'.

- Discuss the apkasa. Explain that it is made from dried coconut palms. What do we use for sifting? Show children a sieve and a colander. Weave with paper.

- Show the children the agbada. Talk about clothes that we wear for special occasions or weddings etc.

- Look at different types of drums. Do they all have circles? Listen to the different sounds. Play different rhythms.

- Show the children the picture of the cowrie shells. Tell the children that they used to be used as money. Paint pasta shells and make necklaces by sticking them on to card and cutting out a necklace shape.

- Cut out a diamond shape. Cut sticky paper into squares and triangles for children to stick on in a pattern. Stick all the diamonds on a length of paper to create a frieze.

- Make two semi-circle clay bowls with self-hardening clay. Show the children how they fit together to make a full circle/sphere.

- Ask the children to look closely at all the pictures – how do the people look different? What else is different? Is anything similar to our lives?

- Look at a plaintain. What does it remind you of? Discuss the fact that it is a vegetable. Taste fried or roasted plaintain.

- Make triangular headdresses. Print designs on them using the different shapes that they have learnt about (possibly using a star fruit!).

- Give the children a shape. Ask them if they can remember what Adaora found that was that shape.

- Go for a walk in the local environment and look for different shapes

Links to themes:

Myself and others

Copyright © 2001 Ifeoma Onyefolu
From "A Triangle for Adaora" by Ifeoma Onyefolu
Reproduced by permission of Frances Lincoln Publishers, London

I'm worried about my little cousin Adaora. She has been behaving strangely. She keeps saying "I really like paw-paw", over and over again.
But when her mother put a slice of paw-paw on Adaora's favourite plate, Adaora just stared at it.
Why won't she eat the paw-paw? If it had been oranges, pineapples or *udala* (a fruit we all love), it would have disappeared very quickly!

A Balloon for Grandad   Nigel Gray and Jane Ray

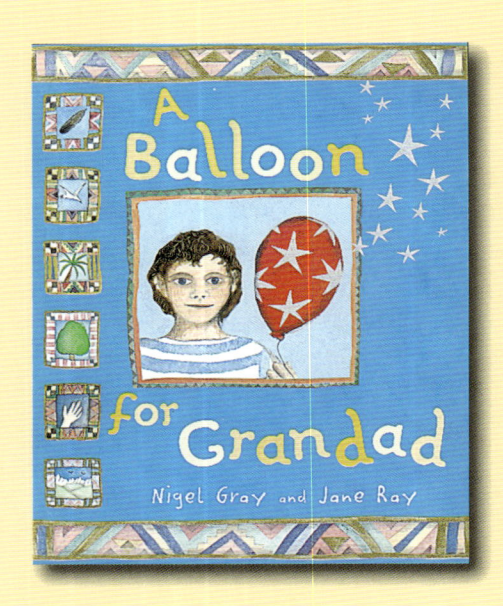

Synopsis

Sam has a big, bright, red balloon. That is, he does until it blows out of the window. But Sam's dad tells him not to be sad, Sam's balloon has gone on an exciting journey across mountains, seas, deserts and rivers, all the way to his grandad Abdulla's house.

ISBN 1-84362-102-9

Questions for discussion:

Why do you think that Sam's grandfather lives in a different country?

Who has a relative in another country? Do you visit that relative or do they visit you?

Why do people move from one place to another?

Has anyone moved from a different country to the UK?

What is grandad Abdulla's house like? How is it different to Sam's home and family?

What do you think you would see if you went to visit grandad Abdulla?

Activities:

- Grandad Abdulla lives on an island in the river Nile in the north of Sudan. Show the children Sudan and the Nile on a map. Show them where the Nile begins and ends.

- Invent a class story about the journey of a balloon. Read **The Blue Balloon** by Mick Inkpen.

- Discuss the differences between Sam's home and grandad Abdulla's home and their lives (e.g. grandad Abdulla tends date trees and looks after goats and lives in a house built of baked mud with a mango tree).

- Give the children a frame (like the pattern in the book). Ask them to draw a picture of a grandparent or close relative. Ask them to describe the person using adjectives.

- Provide trays filled with mud and water. The children can mix the contents together and try to make shapes with the mixture. The shapes should be left to dry in a warm place.

- Show the children a mango. Describe it on the outside – shape, colour, texture, soft, hard, heavy, light etc. Peel off the skin. Describe the inside. Look at the stone from the mango. Taste the fruit or try mango juice. Look closely at dates.

- Give the children a cut-out balloon shape which they can decorate. Ask them to tell the story of its journey. This may relate to a member of their family or a friend who lives far away. Who would they like to send it to? Why?

- Tell the story of the journey of a mango from Africa to our kitchen. Use pictures and props such as a toy aeroplane, a truck, a picture of mango trees, a supermarket and a world map.

- Create a group painting of grandad Abdulla's island or paint the background and each child can paint a house, a tree, a goat etc. to stick on the island.

Links to themes:

My home
My family
Food
Journeys

Copyright © 2002 Nigel Gray and Jane Ray
From "A Balloon for Grandad" by Nigel Gray and Jane Ray
Reproduced by permission of Orchard Books, London

But Martin   June Counsel

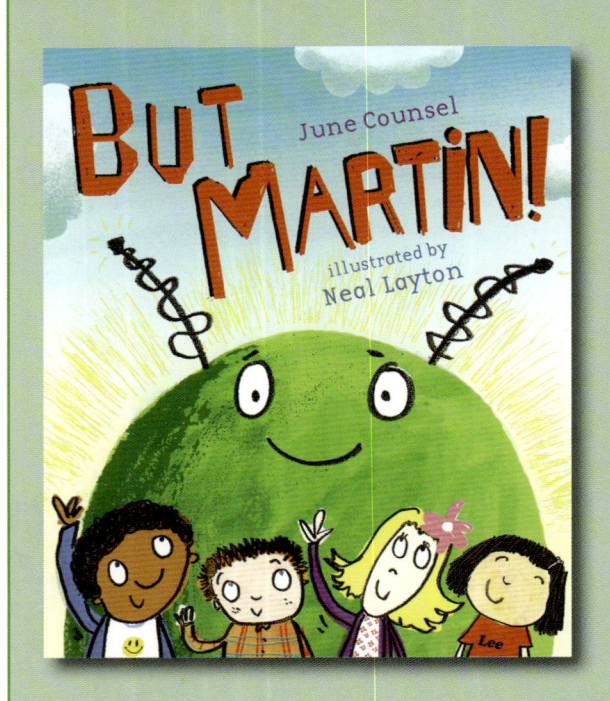

Synopsis

Four very different children are reluctantly making their way to school when they meet Martin. Martin is even more different - he is a green Martian - but they all become great friends.

ISBN 0-552-52312-7

Questions for discussion:

How do you feel when you come to school?
How could we help Angela?
What is different about each character?
Are we like any of the characters in any way?
What makes people the same? Different?
What is Martin like?
How might he feel?
How do you think Martin felt when the children were negative towards him?
How do we show that we are friendly to someone who is different?

Activities:

- Provide 'alien' dressing up clothes in the role-play area.

- Make aliens from playdough, junk modelling materials – ask children to describe them. Look at their similarities and differences.

- Make flying saucers using paper plates, silver foil and other junk modelling materials.

- Change the role play area into a spaceship with a door using cardboard and silver foil. Provide the children with a selection of 'alien' dressing-up clothes. Encourage children to welcome others into the spaceship.

- Use a Persona doll to introduce the children to a new member of the class or setting. Ask the children to think about how to make him/her welcome. This may be developed in the next session. The doll may have experienced a child being unfriendly towards him or her, or may be unhappy for some reason. The children can explore ways to make the doll feel happier.

- Look at the ideas in the chapter on 'Myself and Others' to develop this theme

- Talk about the idea of 'Welcome' and welcoming the stranger. What can we do to make new children and visitors feel welcome?

- Read **It came from Outer Space** by Tony Bradman and Carolyn Wright where the alien is a human being and the children are a class of aliens.

Links to themes:

Myself and others
Journeys

Copyright © 2005 June Counsel
From "But Martin" by June Counsel
Reproduced by permission of Corgi Books, London

Elmer   David McKee

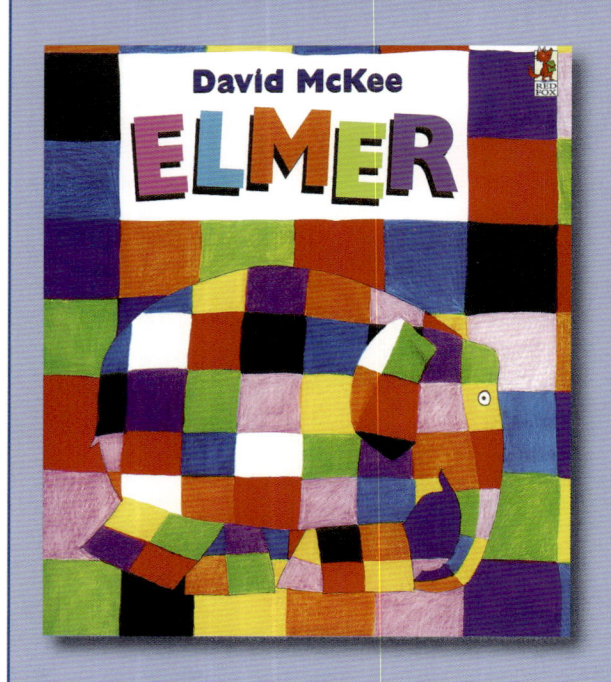

Synopsis

Elmer is not like the rest of the elephants in the jungle, he's a multi-coloured patchwork elephant! In this story, Elmer discovers that his friends laugh at him, not because he's different but because he's the most happy-go-lucky and ever-so-appealing, loveable elephant in the world!

ISBN 0-09-969720-3

Questions for discussion:

Describe how all the grey elephants are different. Encourage language with opposites such as; thin, fat, tall, short, young, old, small, big. Ask the children to look at themselves in this way.

Describe how Elmer is different.

Do you think it is hard to be different like Elmer?

Can you think of another example of a difference like this?

Have you ever laughed at anybody because they are different?

Why did Elmer feel as he did at certain points in the story?

Activities:

- Children create their own 'Elmer'. This could be an ICT activity or painting activity. Their 'Elmer' can be spotty, striped, only two colours, as long as it is not a grey elephant. The children can then describe their own 'Elmer' and look at how they are all different. (See the pictures of the elephants at the end of the story).

- Bring in a toy Elmer or an ordinary elephant that is a cuddly toy. The ordinary elephant can be Elmer covered in the grey berries. Allow the children to ask Elmer questions, for example, Why did you want to be like the other elephants?

- Elmer is a very special elephant. Ask the children to say what they think is special about each of them or to say something special about the child sitting next to them.

- See activities in the chapter 'Myself and Others'

- Find out about African and Indian elephants. Show the children pictures and tell them about the differences and similarities between the elephants.
  Tell them about Africa and India

Links to themes:

Myself and others

Copyright © David McKee
From "Elmer" by David McKee
Reproduced by permission of Random House Books, London

Emeka's Gift   Ifeoma Onyefolu

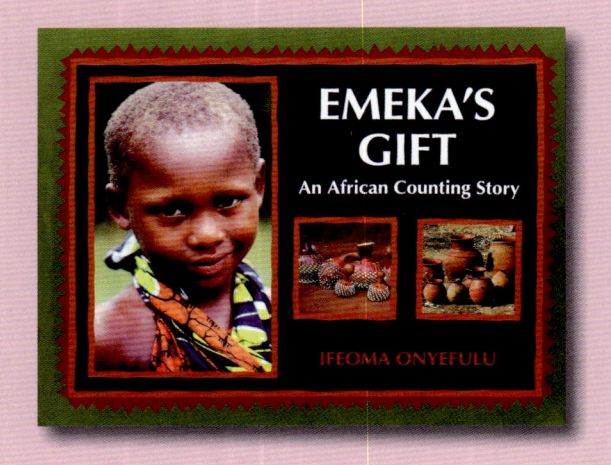

Synopsis

Emeka sets off to visit his grandmother in the next village. He would like to buy her a special present and on the way he looks at all kinds of things, from six beautiful beaded necklaces to nine pestles and mortars.

ISBN 0-7112-1255-4

Questions for discussion:

What does the front cover tell us about this story?

How is Emeka's home different to ours?

How is Emeka's life different to ours?

What are the similarities between us and Emeka?

Who is important in our families? Who is important in Emeka's family?

Activities:

- Find Africa on a world map/globe. Find Nigeria. Find the UK. Where are we in relation to Africa?

- Tell the children more about the Igala tribe. (see the note from the author)

- Front cover - describe Emeka. Does Emeka look like you? Look at his hair, skin colour, clothes. What is similar? What is different?

- Spinning tops – ask children to bring in different types of spinning tops. Look at them, describe them, how they work. Play with them.

- Make a spinning top. (Cut out a circle of card. Children decorate brightly. Push a short pencil through the centre and spin.)

- Make a numberline – one boy, two friends, three women. Children draw/paint pictures. Create a numberline about the children in the setting.

- Look closely at the pictures of people carrying things on their heads. Get children to have a go.

- Do we have markets? What do markets here sell?

- Orange and mango trees – why are they grown in Nigeria? Why can't we grow them here? Bring in mangos and oranges. Describe them on the outside – shape, colour, texture, soft, hard, heavy, light etc. Peel off the skin. Describe the inside. Look at the stone from the mango, pips from the orange – different sizes.
  Make a fruit salad with the 2 fruits.
  Make fruit smoothie with the fruits. Explain how to make it.
  Draw a cross-section of an orange.
  Print with an orange cut in half.

- Beaded necklaces – make necklaces using painted pasta or coloured paper rolled up. Sequence colours. Display on silhouette of face, neck and shoulders. Compare different lengths of the necklaces.

- Ishaka – What is a gourd? Show the children an Ishaka.

- Water pots – talk to the children about dry and rainy seasons – why water needs to be stored. Make clay pots using self-hardening clay.

- Pestle and mortar – show children a pestle and mortar. Get children to try out grinding different types of foods – spices, biscuits etc. Put a pestle and mortar in the home corner.

- Cousins – what is a cousin? Who has cousins? What are their names? How old are they? Where do they live? Look at the picture of Emeka's cousins? Is it a happy picture? Why?

- Family – Why is Emeka the 'best present of all'? Ask the children to talk about grandparents, why they are so special. Talk about family and the generations – children, parents, grandparents and perhaps great-grandparents.

Links to themes:

My family
My home
Myself and others

Copyright © Ifeoma Onyefolu
From "Emeka's Gift" by Ifeoma Onyefolu
Reproduced by permission of Frances Lincoln Publishers, London

Handa's Hen Eileen Browne

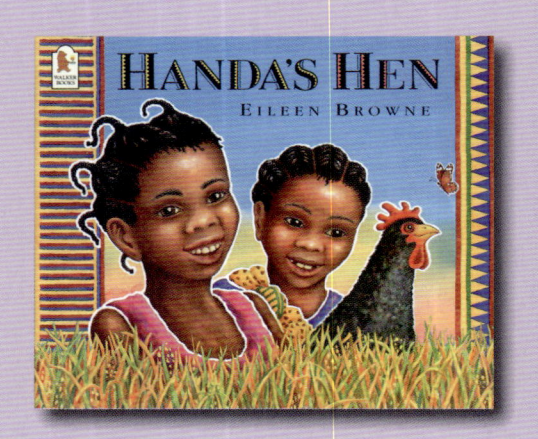

Synopsis

When Handa and her friend Akeyo go looking for Grandma's black hen Mondi, they find two fluttery butterflies round the hen house, three stripey mice under the grain store, four little lizards behind the pots... But where is Mondi? This book provides a global dimension, allowing children to see a snapshot of life in a Kenyan village, but also gives them the opportunity to look at similarities between life here and there.

ISBN 0-7445-9815-X

Questions for discussion:

What does the front cover tell us about this story?
How is Handa's home different to our homes?
How is Handa's life different to ours?
What are the similarities between us and Handa? – loves her grandmother, likes exploring, loves animals, has a best friend.

Activities:

It is important to tell the children that Handa lives in a village in the countryside and that many Kenyan people live in cities and live in buildings like we do, otherwise they are likely to have a distorted view of life in Africa.

- Talk to the children about places far away. Who has been on an aeroplane? Where to? Who has family in another country? Where? Talk about Africa and Kenya. Find Africa on a map or globe. Find South West Kenya.

- Read the story to the children, paying close attention to the pictures and new vocabulary (e.g. illustration on first page tells us so much)
What Handa looks like and what she wears (and other characters)
What Handa does – feed animals
What the village is like, the animals, plants, crops that are growing, climate etc.
Living so near to her grandma
What would the children like to do if they lived in this village?

- Discuss similarities and differences between Handa and the children in your class
  Colour of skin
  Hair style
  Clothes
  Homes/environment – look at the animals, the water hole, farming
  Love of animals
  Closeness of/relationship with grandparents (also see **Grandmother and I** by Helen Buckley and **Emeka's gift** by Ifeoma Onyefulu)
  Theme of families

- Opportunities for counting, make sets of the animals, count them, find more or less, ordering.

- Make a wall display of Handa's village with all the animals and numbers.

- Tell the children more about the unusual animals.

- Look at pattern in clothing, show the children other African prints/fabrics, printing, repeating patterns.

- Display of Handa and Akeyo's journey to find Mondi.

- Print on fabric using sponges or other materials.

- Cut out dress shapes for children to print on. Put silhouette of a face and neck on the dress.

- Make clay pots using self-hardening clay.

- Act out the story with props or pictures.

- What is a grain store? What are the clay pots used for? What is a water hole?

- Handa's breakfast – what might it be? What do we eat for breakfast? Make the two different breakfasts. Compare. Discuss.

- How is Handa's day similar/different to ours? What do you think her school is like? What games do you think she plays?

- Make a counting book or posters of all the animals that the children can then order. Ask the children questions – how many spoonbills?. How many chicks? Recite the numberline.

Links to themes:

Myself and others
My family
My home
Food

Copyright © 2002 Eileen Browne
From "Handa's Hen" by Eileen Browne
Reproduced by permission of Walker Books Ltd, London, SE11 5HJ

Rhymes, songs and poems

Poems

I Like Me!

Sometimes I wish I was someone else,
But mostly I'm glad I'm ME!
We all have our likes and differences as everyone can see.
Some of us like to hurry.
Some like to take our time.
Some are good at English.
Some are good at maths.
Some of us like showers.
Some prefer the bath.
Some of us are quiet.
Some of us are loud.
Some of us like to be alone.
Some of us like a crowd.
Some of us are tall.
Some of us are short.
Some like to play an instrument.
Some like to play a sport.
Some of us are black or brown,
And some of us are white.
Some of us leave the light on
When we go to bed at night.
All of us are special
As everyone can see.
You like you, and I like you,
But also I like ME!

Special

Sung to: "Are You Sleeping?"

I am special,
I am special,
Look at me,
Look at me.
A very special person,
A very special person

That is me, that is me.

One Single Colour

Wouldn't it be terrible? Wouldn't it be sad?
If just one single colour was the colour that we had?
If everything was purple? Or red? Or blue? Or green?
If yellow, pink, or orange was all that could be seen?
Can you just imagine how dull the world would be
If just one single colour was all we got to see?

98

I am Me

No one looks
The way I do
I have noticed
That it's true
No one walks the way I walk
No one talks the way I talk
No one plays the way I play
No one says the things I say
I am special
I am me
There's no one else I'd rather be.

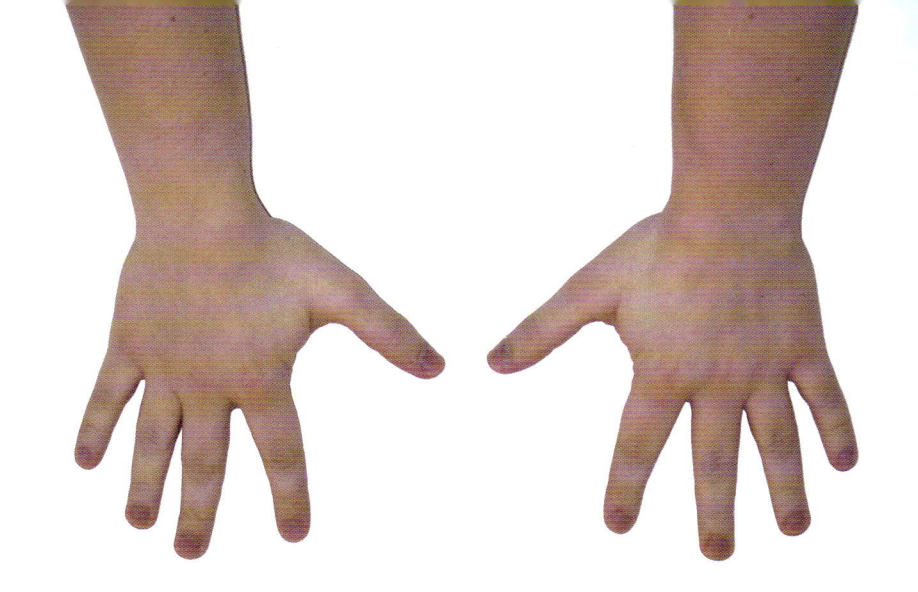

My Head

This is the circle that is my head
This is my mouth with which words are said
These are my eyes with which I see
This is my nose that is part of me
This is the hair that grows on my head
And this is me asleep in my bed.

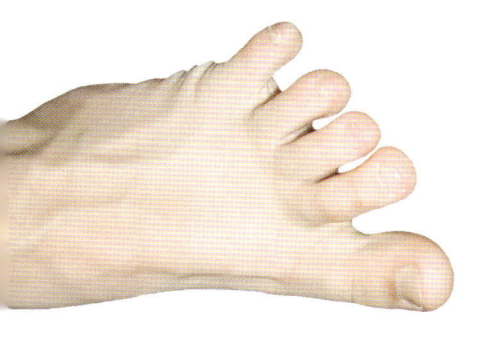

You and Me

I am different from my head to my toes
I am different from my eyes to my nose
I am different, just look at my hair
I am different, you are dark and I am fair
I am different, my face is quite round
I am different, yours is quite square
We are all very different as you can see
But still, we are quite similar
You and me.

Ten fingers

I have ten little fingers,
And they all belong to me.
(hold hands out in front)

I can make them do things,
Would you like to see?
I can shut them up tight.
(make a fist)

I can open them up wide.
(spread fingers out)

I can put them together.
(clasp hands together)

I can make them all hide.
(put hands behind back)

I can make them jump high.
(raise hands over head)

I can make them jump low.
(lower hands to knees)

I can fold them like this
And hold them just so.
(fold hands in lap)

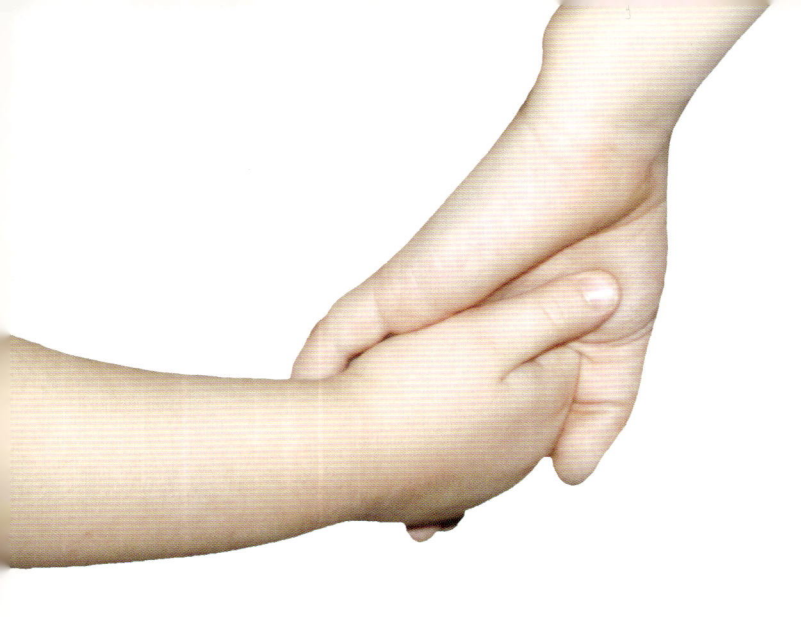

Will you be a friend of mine?

Will you be a friend of mine
Friend of mine
Friend of mine?
Will you be a friend of mine
And (*dance**) around with me?

_____ is a friend of mine
Friend of mine, friend of mine
_____ is a friend of mine
Who (*dance**) around with me.

Change dance for different actions such as, jump, turn, walk

Stand up and take a bow

If your name begins with the letter A
Stand up! Stand up!
If your name begins with the letter B
Stand up! Stand up!
If your name begins with the letter F
Stand up and take a bow.

If your name begins with ABC
Stand up! Stand up!
If your name begins with DEF
Stand up and get in line

(repeat for all letters, combine and mix letters - good for getting children to line up etc.)

Names

(using names)
(to the tune of *Frere Jacques*)

Stand up _____ Stand up _____
Stand up _____ Stand up _____
Reach up very high now
Reach up to the sky now
Then sit down, then sit down.

Songs

Substitute the word *hello* for hello in other languages.

Shalom (Hebrew), Jambo (Swahili), Ciao (Italian)
Hola (Spanish), Merhaba (Turkish), Salaam (Arabic)
www.travlang.com/languages/search.html
has hello and other greetings in many languages.

Hello everyone

Hel-lo ev'ry-one, hel-lo, hel-lo ev'ry-one, hel-lo, hel-lo ev'ry one, hel-lo hel-lo ev'ry-one, hel-lo!

Replace the word 'everyone' with children's names.

Hello everyone,
Hello, hello, everyone
Hello, hello, everyone
Hello, hello, everyone
Hello.

Hello

Hel-lo, how are you? Hel-lo, how are you? Good to see you a-gain, good to see you my friend. Hel-lo, hel-lo, hel-lo!

Hello how are you?
Hello how are you?
Good to see you again
Good to see you my friend
Hello, hello

Hello you!

Fast, happy feel (♩=c.170)

Hel-lo you,_ hel-lo me,_ hel-lo ab-so-lute-ly ev'-ry-bo-dy here, give a cheer,_ make it clear that you're pleased to see your friends to-day! Let's all play,_ have some fun and sing and dance when you sing this song: it won't take long, let the word know you're hap-py and then they'll all smile too!_ Cos if you've got a smile on your face, the whole world_ is a hap-pi-er place!_

* on the repeat, the first two bars can be repeated ad lib., replacing the words 'you' and 'me' with the names of children in the class: hello Jack, hello Jill etc.

Hello you, hello me
Hello absolutely everybody here,
Give a cheer, make it clear
That you're pleased to see your friends to day!

Lets all play
Have some fun and sing and dance
When you sing this song it won't take long,
Let the world know you're happy and then
They'll all smile too!
Cos if you've got a smile on your face,
The whole world is a happier place!

How many ways?

Hel - lo, hel - lo, how ma - ny ways are there to say hel - lo?

Hel - lo, hel - lo, glad to see you my friend.

Hello, hello,
How many ways are there to say hello?
Hello, hello glad to see you my friend.

Imagine a World

♩=c.120

I-magine a world that is just black and white, No col-ours at all,___ what a ter-rible sight___ How bor-ing it would be (how bor-ing it would be) Can't you see?_ We want a rain-bow world. I-mag-ine a world where we all look the same, No diff'rence at all___ what a ter-ri-ble shame, How bor-ing it would be (how bor-ing it would be) can't you see? We want a rain-bow world. Let's put the blue in the sky, let the col-ours fly Let's add the yel-low, or-ange, pink and green___ and as for you and me

© Tamar Andrusier 2006

can't you see? to-geth-er we're a mul-ti-col-oured rain-bow team No mat-ter what your shape or size What-ev-er col-our hair or skin or eyes We are the hum-an race (we are the hum-an race) We share this spe-cial place, We love our rain-bow world. Rain-bow world, we love our rain-bow world. Rain-bow world, we love our rain-bow world.

Imagine a World

Imagine a world
That is just black and white,
No colours at all,
What a terrible sight
How boring it would be,
Can't you see?
We want a rainbow world.

Imagine a world
Where we all look the same,
No difference at all
What a terrible shame,
How boring it would be,
(how boring it would be,)
Can't you see?
We want a rainbow world.

Let's put the blue in the sky,
Let the colour fly.
Let's add the yellow or orange,
Pink and green and as for you and me,
Can't you see?
Together we're a multi-coloured
Rainbow team.

No matter what your shape or size,
Whatever colour hair or skin or eyes,
We are the human race,
(we are the human race)
We share this special place
We love our rainbow world,
Rainbow world,
We love our rainbow world,
We love our rainbow world.

Shalom Haverim

Shalom haverim,
Shalom haverim,
Shalom,
Lehitraot, lehitraot,
Shalom, Shalom!

Shalom, shalom
May peace be with you
Throughout your days,
May peace be with you
Through all that you do,
Shalom, shalom!

Resources

Books

FICTION

Nicholas Allan	**You're all Animals**, Hutchinson Books, 2000	
Bernard Ashley	**Cleversticks**, Picture Lions, 2002	
Floella Benjamin	**Skip Across the Ocean**, Frances Lincoln, 1998	
Eric Carle	**Why Noah Chose the Dove**, Macmillan 1998	
Kathryn Cave & Chris Riddell	**Something Else**, Puffin, 1995	
June Counsel	**But Martin**, Corgi, 2005	
Emma Damon	**All Kinds of People**, Tango Books, 1995	
Emma Damon	**All Kinds of Bodies**, Tango Books, 2002	
Claudia Fries	**A Pig is Moving in**, Siphano Picture Books, 2000	
Tessa Garlake	**Your World, My World**, Oxfam, 2001	
Sheila Hamanaka	**All the Colours of the Earth**, Mulberry Books, 1999	
Beatrice Hollyer	**Wake Up World**, Frances Lincoln, 1999	
Bell Hooks	**Skin Again**, Jump at the Sun, 2005	
Robert G Intrater	**Two Eyes, a Nose and a Mouth**, Scholastic, 1994	
A & B Kindersley	**Children Just Like Me**, Dorling Kindersley, 1995	
Rob Lewis	**Friends**, Henry Holt, 2001	
Debbie Mackinnon	**All About Me**, Frances Lincoln, 2000	
Eric Maddern	**The Fire Children**, Frances Lincoln, 1994	
Mercer Mayer	**Just a Little Different**, Golden Books, 2001	
Peter Nickl	**The Story of the Kind Wolf**, North-South Books, 1996	
David McKee	**Two Monsters**, Red Fox, 1983	
David McKee	**Tusk Tusk**, Red Fox, 1987	
David McKee	**Elmer**, Red Fox, 1990	
Todd Parr	**Black and White**, Megan Tingley Books, 2004	
Todd Parr	**The Peace Book**, Megan Tingley Books, 2004	
Todd Parr	**The Family Book**, Megan Tingley Books, 2004	
Todd Parr	**It's Okay to be Different**, Megan Tingley Books, 2004	
Sandra L Pinkney	**Shades of Black**, Cartwheel Books, 2006	
Dr Seuss	**The Sneetches**, Random House, 2003	
Natasha Tarpley	**I Love my Hair**, Little Brown and Co, 2003	
Evelien Van Dort	**Am I really different?**, Floris Books, 1998	
Max Velthuijs	**Frog and the Stranger**, Anderson Press, 1993	
Jeanne Willis	**Long Blue Blazer**, Red Fox, 2002	
Melanie Walsh	**My Nose, Your Nose**, Corgi, 2005	
Melanie Walsh	**My World, Your World**, Corgi, 2005	

Counting Books

Valerie Bloom	**Fruits - A Caribbean Counting Poem**,	Macmillan, 1997
Faustin Charles	**Caribbean Counting Book**,	Barefoot Books, 1997
Muriel I Feelings	**Moja means One: Swahili Counting Book**,	Puffin 1976
Cathryn Fallwell	**Feast For Ten**,	Houghton Mifflin, 2003
Meg Girnis	**123 for You and Me**,	Albert Whitman and Co, 2000
Brita Granstrom	**Many Hands Counting Book**,	Walker Books, 1998
Lauri Krebs	**We all went on Safari: A Counting Journey through Tanzania**,	Barefoot, 2004
Emily Sper	**Hanukah: A Counting Book in English, Hebrew and Yiddish**,	Cartwheel, 2003
Claudia Zaslavsky	**Counting on Your Fingers African Style**,	Tricycle Press, 2001

Websites

www.qca.org.uk/301.html
QCA - Respect for all: valuing diversity and challenging racism through the curriculum
Ideas and lesson plans for all areas of the curriculum

www.under5s.co.uk
Ideas for nursery settings on many topics including festivals and special days

www.support4learning.org.uk/sites/support4learning/religious_calendars/religious_calendars.cfm
Links to up-to-date calendar of festivals

www.antiracisttoolkit.org.uk
Practical ideas to promote race equality, case studies and materials for staff training

www.mamalisa.com/world
Children's songs and nursery rhymes from around the world

www.multicultural-art.co.uk
Multicultural posters for all ages

www.cafod.org.uk/resources/schoolsteachers
Resources for global citizenship

www.unicef.org.uk/tz/resources/index.asp
Useful resources about children's rights

www.dep.org.uk
Excellent resources on race equality and global citizenship

www.willesdenbookshop.co.uk
Willesden Bookshop. Specialises in multicultural books

www.jcore.org.uk
Resources, training and workshops on race equality

www.oxfam.org.uk/coolplanet/
Ideas and resources for teaching about global citizenship

www.open-sez-mefestivals.co.uk
Resources for multicultural learning

Resources for practitioners

Redvers Brandling and Barbara Cass-Beggs	**Every Colour Under the Sun**, Ward Lock Educational, 1983
Margaret Collins	**Circle Time for the Very Young**, Lucky Duck Publishing
Carole Court	**Multicultural Activities**, Scholastic, 2000
Geoff Davies	**We are Family**: An Assembly Book for 4-8 year olds, Nash Pollock publishing, 2000
Opal Dunn	**Acker Backa Boo! Games to say and play from around the world**, Frances Lincoln, 2000
Emily Feldberg and Rob Walton	**Ideas for Citizenship(KS1)**, Scholastic, 2002
Sandip Hazareesingh	**Speaking about the Past: Oral History for 5-7 year olds**, Trentham Books, 1994
Eleanor Knowles and Wendy Ridley	**Another Spanner in the works: Challenging Prejudice and Racism in Mainly White Schools**, Trentham Books, 2005
Runnymede Trust	**The Runnymede Trust Complementing Teachers: A Practical guide to Promoting Race Equality in Schools**, Runnymede, 2003
Mary Young and Eilish Commins	**Global Citizenship: The Handbook for Primary Teaching**, Oxfam, 2002
Angela Wood	**Homing In: A Practical Resource for Religious Education**, Trentham Books, 1998

Catalogues

Barefoot Books – celebrating art and story with books that open the hearts and minds of children from all walks of life
www.barefootbooks.com
01903 82800

Letterbox Library – celebrating equality and diversity in the best children's books
Book packs for nurseries available
www.letterboxlibrary.com
020 7503 4801

The Festival Shop – for Multifaith, Multicultural and Citizenship resources
www.festivalshop.co.uk
0121 444 0444

Mantra Lingua – dual-language creative learning resources
www.mantralingua.com
01204 366868

Multicultural Resources – early years catalogue contains books, puzzles, music, dolls and clothes
www.multicultural-resources.com
01204 366868

Eduzone – resources for early years
www.eduzone.co.uk
08456 445556

Oxfam Catalogue for Schools
www.oxfam.org.uk
01202 712933

Parrotfish – multicultural resources and artefacts
www.parrotfish.co.uk

Starbeck Education Resources – vast array of artefacts from around the world including music and textiles
www.starbeck.com
01765 607815

Religion in Evidence – books and artefacts on major world religions
www.tts-shopping.com
0800 318686

Early Years Equality – working to promote race equality in the field of early years provision.
www.earlyyearsequality.org

Background information - books and articles

Babette Brown	**Unlearning discrimination in the early years**, Trentham Books, 1998
Babette Brown	**Combating discrimination: Persona Dolls in Action**, Trentham Books, 2005
Commission for Racial Equality	**Learning for All: Standards for Racial Equality in Schools**, 2002
L. Derman Sparks	**Anti-Bias Curriculum: Tools for Empowering Young Children**, NAEYC, Washington, USA, 1998. Available from National Children's Bureau
Early Years Equality	**A Policy for Excellence: Developing a Policy for Excellence**: Developing a Policy for Equality in Early Years Settings, 2001
Jane Lane	**Action for racial equality in the early years: Understanding the past, thinking about the present, planning for the future** National Early Years Network, 1999 Available from the National Children's Bureau
Jane Lane	**Dealing with Prejudice and Discrimination: the Issues and in Practice** Practical Pre-School, Issue 2, 2001
Pre-school Learning Alliance	**Equal Chances: Eliminating Discrimination and Ensuring Equality in Pre-school Settings**, 2001
R Richardson and A Wood	**Inclusive Schools: Inclusive Society: Race and Identity on the Agenda**, Race on the Agenda in partnership with Association of London Government and Save the Children, 1999
Runnymede Trust	**Complementing Teachers: A Practical Guide to Promoting Race Equality in Schools**, 2003
Save the Children	**Anti-Bias approaches in the Early Years**, 2000

Save the Children	**Home from Home: A Guidance and Resource Pack for the Welcome and Inclusion of Refugee Children and Families in School**, Save the Children, Salusbury World, 2004
I Siraj-Blatchford	**The Early Years: Laying the Foundations for Racial Equality**, Trentham Books, 1994

Multicultural music

Putumayo	**African Playground** An entertaining and educational musical expedition to Africa
Putumayo	**Caribe! Caribe!** Caribbean journey
Putumayo	**Carnival** Upbeat songs from many of the world's great carnival celebrations
Putumayo	**Dreamland** Lullabies and soothing songs from around the world
Putumayo	**World Playground 1 and 2** CDs that take children on an inspiring musical, cultural journey Around the globe
Helen MacGregor & Baoobie Gargrave	**Let's Go Zudie-o** – Book and CD Creative activities for dance and music

Personal resources

From Policy to Practice

Race Equality Policy

> This policy has been written from the perspective of a Jewish nursery.
> However, it may be used as a template for any nursery by changing or taking
> out the sections or statements in bold text.

Background information:

Describe the catchment area of the nursery, the community that it serves.
Describe the type of nursery: private, synagogue etc.
Describe the composition of the nursery, i.e. children who have English as an additional language, ethnic backgrounds etc.

You may wish to use an appropriate Torah quote here, for example, "Tzedek, tzedek tirdof-" "Justice, justice shall you pursue" (Deut. 16:20)

We are aware that as a Jewish nursery, we have a key role to play in eradicating racism and valuing diversity. We aim to put into practice the values that are embedded within the teachings of Judaism with an understanding that all nurseries and schools have an important role to play in increasing mutual understanding, respect and appreciation of cultural diversity.

This Race Equality Policy enables ………………………… nursery to meet its statutory obligations under the Race Relations (Amendment) Act 2000 to:
- Eliminate unlawful racial discrimination
- Promote equal opportunities
- Promote good relations between people of different racial groups

Aims:

- To value diversity and promote equality.
- To strive to ensure that everyone in the setting is treated with respect and that children learn to respect others outside of the setting.
- To promote race equality and oppose racism in all its forms and foster positive attitudes and commitment to an education for equality.
- To prepare children in the setting for life in a multicultural society.
- To encourage children to appreciate the benefits of diversity.
- To build an inclusive environment, where every child can fulfil their potential.

We aim to achieve this by:

- Creating an ethos which fosters respect, team spirit, responsibility and cooperation.
- Encouraging everyone within our nursery to participate in all aspects of nursery life and feel valued.
- Promoting mutual respect and valuing a variety of contributions and skills from our children, teachers, parent body and the wider community.
- Identifying and removing all practices, procedures and customs which are discriminatory and replacing them with positive activities and resources which promote inclusion.
- Using a race equality audit to establish the nursery's current practice and setting targets to determine the way forward. These will be monitored and reviewed regularly.

Nursery staff should:

- Integrate race equality within the development planning of the nursery.
- Ensure that information to parents is in a format accessible to ALL parents.
- Promote equality and fairness in all aspects of their work.
- Respond appropriately to racism and racist incidents as and when they occur.
- Deliver a curriculum which acknowledges and celebrates diversity.

Curriculum:

- **Children are taught about respect and tolerance through Jewish values.**
- All children are given opportunities to explore issues of race equality and diversity in the curriculum.
- Children feel that their own background is acknowledged and valued in the nursery.
- An anti-racist approach permeates the whole curriculum and anti-discriminatory practices are in place.
- Circle time is used as an opportunity to discuss issues pertaining to race equality.

Development and learning through play:

- An anti-racist learning environment is provided.
- Opportunities for planning multicultural and anti-racist education are used well.
- A range of regularly updated resources contribute to creating a culturally diverse environment.
- The diversity of the children in the nursery and the local community is used effectively.

Support for children and families:

- Children are aware that racist behaviour will not be tolerated in the nursery.
- Support is given to children who encounter racial discrimination or harrassment.
- Children who display racist behaviour are given support in addressing their behaviour and attitudes.
- Parents are involved where a child displays racist behaviour or is a victim of racial harassment.
- Children demonstrate a positive attitude towards people who are different from themselves.
- **The nursery actively promotes and values diversity including bilingualism and children from different Jewish backgrounds, for example Ashkenazi or Sephardi, or different levels of observance.**

Ethos:

- Children who demonstrate a positive attitude towards others are visibly valued and praised.
- Ethnic, cultural and linguistic diversity is recognised, valued and promoted as a positive feature of the setting.
- Displays, resources and other material around the setting recognise and promote diversity.
- **Within and outside the Jewish community diversity is recognised as having a positive role to play within the setting, i.e. challenging racism and recognising diversity, provides the Jewish community with a better understanding of its place in contemporary British society.**

Resources:

- Diversity is celebrated in the ethos of the nursery, through displays of children's work and through evidence of links to local minority ethnic communities and groups.
- The setting has good resources for teaching about diversity, including books, toys, artefacts and posters.
- Fair recruitment practices are evident.

This Race equality policy was formally adopted by (name of setting)
Date......................

Adapted from 'Developing a Nursery Policy for Race Equality' – Centre for Race Equality, Scotland)

AUDIT
Race Equality Practice Across The Foundation Stage Curriculum

All areas of learning and subject areas contain opportunities for teaching directly or indirectly about race equality and cultural diversity. Here are some of the many possibilities. Use the grid to comment on each section. This will reveal the areas that need to be targeted in your action plan.

1. IN PLAY

1. The resources in the home corner are culturally diverse. At times there is a specific focus on a particular culture/community (eg an Asian/White home, a Chinese or Caribbean grocery store etc.).

2. Dressing up clothes, dolls, puppets, 'Duplo' and toys generally are culturally diverse.

3. Situations are created in structured play to explore issues of cultural diversity, including racism.

4. Opportunities are taken in unstructured play to explore issues concerning cultural diversity, including racism.

5. Children are encouraged to voice their opinions, discuss with others and work together in solving problems concerning cultural diversity, including racism.

2. PERSONAL, SOCIAL AND EMOTIONAL DEVELOPMENT

1. Practitioners and other adults provide a range of positive role models from a variety of communities.

2. Positive images are used, for example, in books and displays that challenge children's thinking.

3. There are opportunities in play and learning that take account of children's particular religious and cultural beliefs.

4. Children are encouraged to develop an awareness, of and sensitivity, to the needs, views and feelings of others.

5. Children are encouraged to value their own cultures and those of other people.

6. Children understand that racist name-calling and racist behaviour is not acceptable and why.

7. Children are encouraged to feel they have a right to have their needs treated with respect by others.

3. PHYSICAL DEVELOPMENT

1. Equipment and other materials reflect diverse racial backgrounds.

2. Pupils are encouraged to participate in and value games, dance, PE and playground activities that reflect diverse racial backgrounds.

3. Schools try to involve community members from diverse racial backgrounds to teach games reflective of their backgrounds.

4. LANGUAGE AND LITERACY

1. Opportunities exist to share and enjoy a wide range of rhymes, poetry, stories and books, which reflect diverse racial backgrounds.

2. Children are encouraged to explore differences within the context of similarities.

3. Imaginative opportunities (e.g. story and Persona dolls) are created for children to talk about racist incidents.

4. Musical and artistic activities reflect diverse racial backgrounds.

5. Opportunities exist for children to hear, use, see and read familiar words in many languages through posters, notices, labels, books, audio and video materials

6. Opportunities exist for children to see adults writing in languages as well as English and to write for themselves.

7. As far as practical, bilingual workers are involved in developing the spoken language of those children who speak English as an additional language.

8. Children are encouraged to use their home language when appropriate and to sing songs that allow them to say hello, goodbye etc. in their home language.

5. KNOWLEDGE AND UNDERSTANDING OF THE WORLD

1. Children's own experiences are considered through different school activities to develop an appreciation of diverse racial backgrounds, e.g. trips, visitors to schools, celebrations, food, clothing, materials etc.

2. A stimulating environment is provided with resources that reflect cultural diversity.

3. Activities exist to encourage the exploration, observation and discussion of issues concerning racial equality and harmony.

4. Opportunities exist to explore similarities, differences and patterns between people from diverse racial backgrounds.

5. The contribution from people from diverse racial backgrounds in the world that we live in is demonstrated in text, pictures, discussion etc.

6. Opportunities exist for pupils to know about their own cultures and beliefs and to learn about those of others.

7. Opportunities exist for pupils to share their knowledge of their own family heritage and that of others.

6. CREATIVE DEVELOPMENT

1. **There is a rich environment, which values creativity and expressiveness across a range of cultures,** including displays, posters, artefacts etc.

2. There is a wide range of activities which reflect cultural diversity.

3. There are resources from different cultures used to stimulate different ways of thinking.

4. There are resources that facilitate the exploration of different identities, such as crayons that reflect accurate skin tones and dolls with different skin tones, physical features, clothing, jewellery etc.

5. Opportunities are provided to work alongside artist, musicians, mime artistes, dancers and other talented adults from a variety of traditions and communities.

6. Activities which are imaginative and enjoyable and encourage seeing things from different points of view are regularly organised.

7. Culturally specific activities are used to enhance and reinforce self-esteem.

8. Explorations of colour, shape, form and space in two and three dimensions use materials which reflect cultural diversity.

9. Song and dance draw on a variety of traditions and cultures.

10. Art and design draw on different cultures in terms of materials and themes.

11. Imaginative role play and stories reflect cultural diversity and also provide opportunities to explore feelings (self and others) about inclusion and exclusion.

7. MATHEMATICAL DEVELOPMENT

1. Diverse racial backgrounds are reflected in the mathematics of counting, sorting and matching activities.

2. Geometric patterns and shapes are used to draw on a range of cultural traditions.

3. Diverse racial backgrounds are reflected in stories, songs, games and imaginative play used in teaching numeracy.

4. Reference is made to a variety of number systems used by people from diverse racial backgrounds.

5. Children who speak English as an additional language are helped in developing and using specifically mathematical language.

8. DIVERSE NEEDS OF CHILDREN

1. There are opportunities to build on, extend and value children's own diverse knowledge, experiences, interests and competencies.

2. A wide range of strategies based on children's language and learning needs are used.

3. A safe and supportive learning environment is provided free from racial harassment.

4. Racial stereotypes are challenged.

5. Materials reflect diversity and are free from discrimination.

9. PARENTS/CARERS AS PARTNERS

1. All parents/carers are welcomed and valued through a range of different opportunities for collaboration between children, parents and practitioners.

2. The knowledge and expertise of parents/carers and other family members should be used to support learning opportunities provided by settings.

3. Practitioners use a variety of ways to keep parents/carers fully informed about the setting's values, including their position on race equality and curriculum, such as: brochures, displays, tapes, videos.

4. Parents/carers are kept fully informed through informal discussion and letters in home languages.

5. Experiences at home, for example, visits and celebrations, are used to develop learning in the school setting. Contributions from parents/carers are encouraged and welcomed,

10. ETHOS OF THE SETTING

1. Multicultural and anti-racist education permeates the whole curriculum, differentiated to meet the needs of all the children.

2. The ethos of the setting is inclusive towards all children in the setting and beyond.

3. Race equality is taken into account in all planning and the implementation of the curriculum as a natural process.

4. Mono-cultural settings reflect the diversity of the UK and consider this in planning, curriculum and resources.

5. There is a whole-nursery approach to issues of equality and fairness which are apparent in the ethos of the setting.

(Adapted from Young, Gifted and Equal: Race Equality Standards for Schools from Leicester City Council 2003, written by, Kamljit Obhi, Clive Billingham and Chino Cabon)

INDICATOR NUMBER	HOW ARE WE DOING? (Examples of good practice)	AREAS FOR DEVELOPMENT	WHAT ASSISTANCE DO WE REQUIRE? (e.g. training, resources)
1.1			

Other JCORE Publications

Let's Make a Difference: Teaching Anti-racism in Primary Schools – A Jewish Perspective by Dr. Edie Friedman, Hazel Woolfson, Sheila Freedman and Shirley Murgraff, Price: £15.00 + £3.00 P&P

This excellent resource can help to tackle the difficult topic of racism, using insights of Jewish teachings and experience. This publication examines ways of preventing and combating stereotyping and racism and will also help to educate young people about issues relating to asylum seekers and refugees.

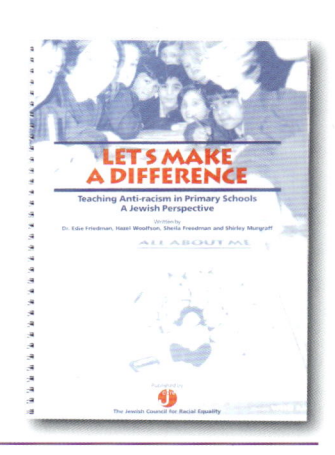

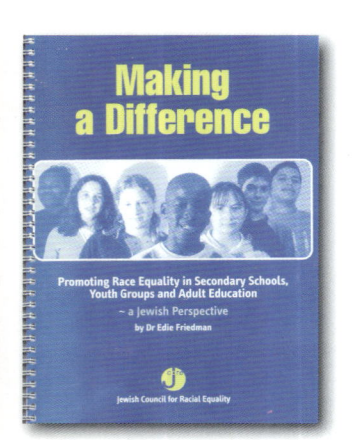

Making a Difference: Promoting Race Equality in Secondary Schools, Youth Groups and Adult Education – A Jewish Perspective
by Dr. Edie Friedman, Price: £15.00 + £3.00 P&P

This book is primarily intended for Jewish children but the content provides an invaluable resource for studying citizenship at Key Stage Three and Four. It examines both the Jewish experiences of racism as well as that of the Black and Asian communities. The background information is concise and accessible with a variety of activities ranging from discussion and role play to practical written activities, all providing a stimulating introduction to the issue of racism.

Unaccompanied Refugee Children: Have the lessons been learnt?
Price: £2.00 + P&P

This booklet examines the treatment of unaccompanied child refugees today using testimonies of the Kindertransport. It provides an insight into the experience of being separated from one's family and thrust into a new culture and an unfamiliar society. There is information about the contemporary experiences of unaccompanied children today and a variety of case studies that describe the plight of refugee children. This booklet also provides ideas for activities and a list of useful contacts.

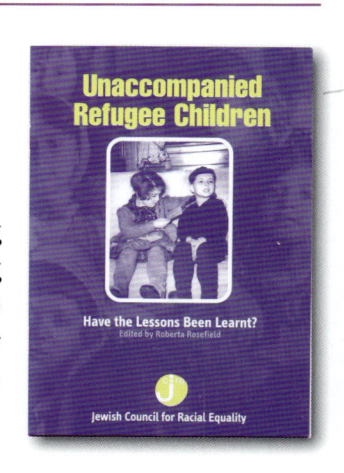

Citizenship Postcards
£5.00 + 0.50 p&p

This series of ten postcards is designed for use by years five to seven. They can be used to stimulate a wide range of activities that link with the QCA schemes of work. They can also be used to discuss active citizenship and ways to promote a better understanding of issues pertaining to equality and diversity.